LAZY COOK® Fans Write!

*"**Lazy Cook** fans come from all professions, all walks of life, all income levels. And they all have one desire in common—to eat well at home and not spend a lot of time doing it."*

— G.P.M, Dallas, Texas

"My husband is 94 years old. He claims your Catfish Parmesan is 'the best fish he has ever eaten!' I'm enjoying trying new recipes again because they aren't too taxing ... people are so busy these days, and your book will help them greatly!"

— S.O., Delray Beach, Florida

*"Being the busy person I am, I love the quick and easy recipes in **The Lazy Cook** book. With this cookbook at hand, preparing food becomes a pleasure, not a chore."*

— F.O., Santa Fe, New Mexico

*"Thank you for writing **The Lazy Cook**. The recipes are interesting, good, and different from the usual cookbooks. I'd like to order five more copies to give to my children for Christmas. The books will be a big help in their busy schedules."*

— J.F., Boca Raton, Florida

"I've finally found a cookbook that rewards my laziness."

— G.J., Manhattan, New York

"Your recipe book is very useful for me. The print is large and the format permits me to read without my glasses."

— R.T., Rantoul, Illinois

*Sure Nature is bountiful, but does that obligate you to slave for hours in preparing meals? Nah! Ten minutes is plenty! Do it **The Lazy Cook®** way.*

The
THE LAZY COOK®

Delicious Recipes That Take Ten Minutes or Less to Prepare

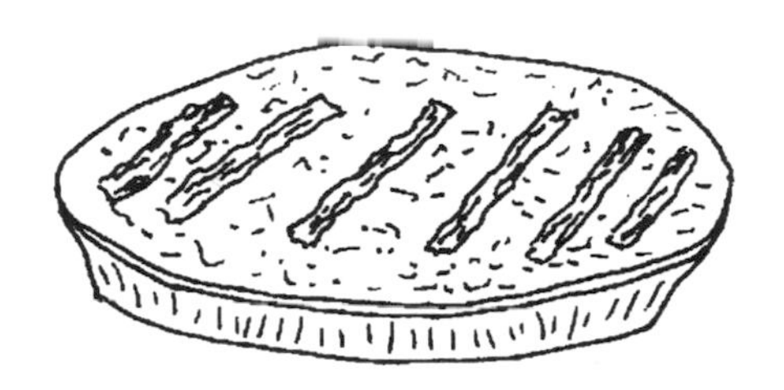

Catherine O. McManus and
Krystyn E. Arnold

Publisher: Ralph Roberts
Executive Editor: Pat Hutchison Roberts

Managing Editor: Vicki Ball
Editors: Kathryn L. Hall, Samuel Garrison, Pat Roberts

Cover Design: **WorldComm®**
Interior Design & Electronic Page Assembly: WorldComm®
Illustrations: Catherine O. McManus

10 9 8 7 6 5 4

Library of Congress Cataloging-in-Publication Data

McManus, Catherine O., 1935-
The lazy cook : delicious recipes that take ten minutes or less to prepare / Catherine O. McManus and Krystyn E. Arnold.
p. cm.
Includes index.
ISBN 1-57090-012-4 (alk. paper)
1. Quick and easy cookery. I. Arnold, Krystyn E., 1953- . II. Title.
TX833.5.M45 1995 95-37210
641.5'55--dc20 CIP

Alexander Books—a division of Creativity, Inc.—is a full–service publisher located at 65 Macedonia Road, Alexander NC 28701. Phone (704) 252–9515, Fax (704) 255–8719.

Alexander Books is distributed to the trade by **Alexander Distributing**, 65 Macedonia Road, Alexander NC 28701. Phone (704) 252–9515, Fax (704) 255–8719. For orders: (800) 472-0438. Visa and MasterCard accepted.

PREFACE

This book is dedicated to all those who love to eat well but do not wish to make a "career" out of cooking. Most of us are extremely busy today and haven't the time our mothers did to prepare delicious, healthy meals. We have found that drive-thru fast-food outlets and greasy take-out menus fill the stomach, but pinch the pocketbook and don't provide adequate nutrition. **The Lazy Cook®** is here to help. The recipes in this book take 10 minutes or less preparation time, leaving you more time for other priorities—be they business or pleasure.

There are several keys to reducing your time in the kitchen in addition to these recipes. Organization of the physical surroundings is crucial, and only you can arrange your work space to be most efficient for the way you work.

We have made our cooking faster by placing our cooking utensils in antique buckets on the counter near the stove. Wooden utensils plus kitchen scissors are on the left and metal and plastic on the right. Removing the doors to the cupboard which houses our pots and pans and stacking the lids in corresponding order with the pots has made their retrieval easier. Our most frequently used pan, the stovetop wok, is within arm's reach of the stove. We disposed of the spice rack in favor of a single-file arrangement of spices across half the cabinet next to the stove. The remaining half of the cabinet houses canned goods. A shelf above the stove is home to grains and pasta in antique canning jars.

Our freezer-top is also stocked for speed and ease of use. Frozen vegetables are stacked three deep on the right with the labels readable from the front. Meat (bagged in most commonly used quantities) fills the area between the vegetables and the ice maker, with infrequently used items under the ice-maker. Partially used bags of vegetables are stored in the door of the freezer.

We keep a variety of sizes of plastic bags, both ziplock and the "old-fashioned" kind, in a drawer to the right of the stove along with various kinds of fasteners. Our favorite fastener looks like a hair barrette and comes in small and large versions. They close everything from bags of frozen hamburger patties to partial bags of frozen vegetables as well as bags of pasta. We couldn't live without them. The drawer to the left of our stove contains a variety of knives along with infrequently used kitchen utensils, stored in interlocking plastic trays. All of our baking pans are on pull-out shelves in the lower cabinet to the right of the stove along with measuring cups, spoons, etc.

Whenever possible we have the most commonly used ingredients for each appliance in a cupboard near that appliance. For instance, the coffee and filters are in the cabinet immediately above the coffee maker. And yes, we do have a bread maker. The flour, sugar, dry milk, and the measuring scoops are stored in the cabinet immediately below it. We are fortunate to have a specially designed cabinet in another room to house most of our dishes. Therefore we can devote our kitchen space primarily to cooking.

The Lazy Cook® is a very versatile book. Most of the recipes are conducive to elegant dining as well as casual. The determining factor is presentation. Eye appeal plays a tremendous role in the enjoyment of food and is important for all occasions. Placing an entree on a bed of greens or garnishing with a colorful vegetable livens up the meal whether it is served on your finest china or your "everyday" pottery. The choice of tablecloth, napkins, napkin rings, dishes, silver, glassware, serving pieces, and centerpiece all play a part.

Dining elegantly does not require taking out a second mortgage on the house. You can find exquisite pieces in the most unexpected places. Antique stores, resale shops, thrift shops, and yard sales are a great place to look for good buys in china, crystal, silver, and linens. Don't be afraid to mix patterns when selecting items. Find patterns that complement each other rather than compete. Centerpieces can be made from natural objects or unusual items in your house. A friend of ours has a hat pin collection which she sometimes incorporates in a centerpiece. Express yourself, but be careful not to interrupt conversation. Be creative when serving your meals and you, as well as those you nurture, will reap the rewards.

A brief example will prove my point. One evening our next door neighbors, who are gourmet cooks, were coming to dinner at 6:00 pm. At 5:30 I walked into the kitchen, sighing and wondering what to prepare. After scanning the refrigerator for ingredients, I had an idea for a new recipe—thus the creation of our recipe "Beef in a Basket." I spent 7 minutes preparing the dish and in the 10 minutes it baked, I microwaved Oriental vegetables and warmed a can of cream of chicken soup for gravy. Catherine shredded some carrots and cabbage for a salad, which she dressed and served on a bed of lettuce. We served coffee with a dash of chocolate for dessert. The chocolate was SWISS MISS sugar-free hot chocolate mix. (They never knew!) The total meal, from start to finish, took us 18 minutes.

We set the table with WEDGEWOOD china, MIKASA crystal, and a mixture of antique silver. The centerpiece consisted of two silver candelabra with white candles surrounded by miniature antique shoes which Catherine's mother collected. We served the "beef baskets" on a WEDGEWOOD platter garnished with sprigs of mint (which just happens to grow outside our back door). A crystal bowl held the vegetables, over which we drizzled our "soup/gravy," then sprinkled with paprika and slivered almonds. The carrot/cabbage salad was served on a bed of lettuce on square WEDGEWOOD salad plates. We ate by candlelight and the meal made an elegant impression...so much so that we were asked for the entree recipe, and "Beef in a Basket" was served to the next nine guests at our neighbors' home.

Time is saved in shopping as well as cooking when you use **The Lazy Cook®**. The recipes use common ingredients and are usually found in your local grocery. The search for exotic spices is eliminated.

We wish you many meals of pleasant cooking and happy eating with **The Lazy Cook®**. Now—if you only had someone to clean up!

KEA

CONTENTS

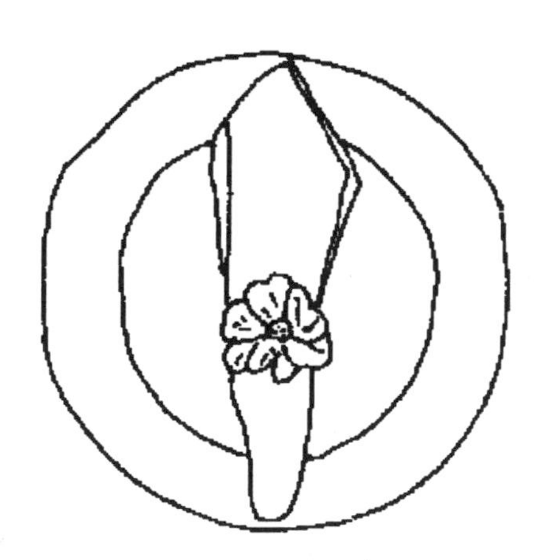

BEEF ENTREES

APPLESAUCE MEATBALLS

A new concept in meatballs!

2 lbs. hamburger
1½ cups applesauce
2 cups corn flakes, crushed
2 eggs, beaten
1 tsp. garlic salt
1 tsp. black pepper

2 cans (10¾ oz. size) tomato soup

Preheat oven to 350 degrees.

Using a non-stick cooking spray, grease a 9 x 13-inch baking dish.

In a large bowl, combine first 6 ingredients.
Mix thoroughly.
Form into 18 balls.
Place in baking dish.

In a bowl, whisk undiluted tomato soup.
Pour soup over meatballs.

Bake (covered) 1 hour.

Serves 6.

MEXICAN MIX

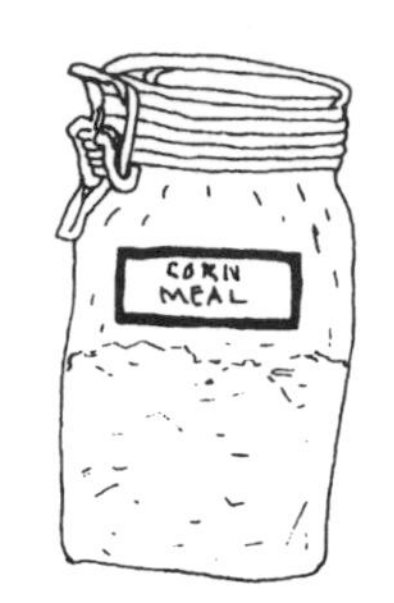

1 lb. hamburger
1 can (8 oz.) tomato sauce
1 pkg. taco seasoning

1 can (16 oz.) refried beans

taco chips

2 cups cheddar cheese, shredded

Preheat oven to 350 degrees.
Grease a 2-qt. casserole dish.

Brown meat and drain.

Mix in 1/2 of tomato sauce and 1/2 of taco seasoning. Set aside.

Mix beans with remaining tomato sauce and taco seasoning.

Layer in dish as follows:
taco chips
meat mixture
bean mixture

Repeat layers.

Bake (uncovered) 25 minutes.

Sprinkle cheese on top.
Bake until cheese melts.

Serves 4-6.

❤

TAMALE PIE

1 lb. hamburger
1 small onion, chopped

1 can (16 oz.) tomato sauce
1 cup milk
2 eggs, beaten
1 can (16 oz.) whole kernel corn, drained
1/2 cup sliced pitted ripe olives
3/4 cup yellow corn meal
1 tsp. chili powder
1/2 tsp. salt
1/2 tsp. black pepper
1/2 tsp. ground red pepper

Preheat oven to 350 degrees.
Using a non-stick cooking spray, grease a 9 x 13-inch baking dish.

In a skillet, brown hamburger and onion.
Drain and turn into a large mixing bowl.

Add remaining ingredients.
Mix thoroughly.
Turn into baking dish.

Bake (uncovered) 45 minutes or until knife inserted in center comes out clean.

Serves 6.

❤

CHILI PIE

1 lb. ground beef
1 small onion, chopped

1 tsp. chili powder
1/4 tsp. cumin
1 tsp. Worcestershire sauce
1 can (16 oz.) stewed tomatoes
1 can (16 oz.) kidney beans, drained

1 pkg. (8½ oz.) cornbread mix

Preheat oven to 425 degrees.
Using a non-stick cooking spray, grease a 9 x 13-inch baking dish.

In a large Dutch oven, saute first 2 ingredients and drain.

Add next 5 ingredients and simmer 15 minutes.

Meanwhile:

Make cornbread mix according to package directions. **Do not bake.**

Turn meat mixture into baking dish.
Spread cornbread batter over top with a wet knife.

Bake (uncovered) 20 minutes.

Serves 6.

BEEF BRIO

1 cup long grain white rice, uncooked
1 cup frozen whole kernel corn, thawed
1 cup tomato sauce
1/2 cup water
1 onion, chopped
1 green pepper, chopped
3/4 lb. ground beef, uncooked and crumbled
1 tsp. black pepper
1/2 tsp. salt
1 cup tomato sauce
1/2 cup water
4 strips bacon, cut in half

Preheat oven to 350 degrees.
Using a non-stick cooking spray, grease a 3-qt. covered casserole dish.

Layer all ingredients in order listed.
Bake (covered) 1 hour.

Bake (uncovered) 30 minutes.

Serves 4.

GROUND BEEF STROGANOFF

1 onion, chopped
2 celery stalks, chopped
2 Tbsp. butter

1 lb. lean ground beef

1/2 cup water
1 tsp. salt
1 tsp. black pepper
1 tsp. lemon pepper
1/2 tsp. basil
1 can (8 oz.) mushrooms

1 can (10¾ oz.) cream of mushroom soup

1 cup sour cream

cooked egg noodles
parsley for garnish

In a large Dutch oven, saute first 2 ingredients in butter.
Add meat and brown.

Drain and return to pan.

Add next 6 ingredients. Cook (on high) 5 minutes.

Add undiluted soup and simmer (uncovered) 10 minutes.

Stir in sour cream.
Heat thoroughly. Do not boil.

Serve over noodles. Garnish with parsley.

Serves 4.

MEAT LOAF

Catherine got this recipe when she was 12 years old from her neighbor.

1 egg
1 cup milk
3 cups corn flakes
1 onion, chopped
1 green pepper, chopped

2 lbs. hamburger
1/2 tsp. salt
1/2 tsp. black pepper
1/4 tsp. garlic powder
1/2 tsp. lemon pepper
1/4 tsp. ground red pepper
1/4 cup catsup

Preheat oven to 375 degrees.

In a large bowl, mix first 5 ingredients.

Add remaining ingredients.
Mix well.
Form into a loaf.
Place in a 9 x 13-inch baking dish.

Bake (uncovered) 1½ hours or until thoroughly cooked.

Serves 6-8.

CHOP SUEY BAKE

1 lb. ground beef
1/2 tsp. salt
1 tsp. black pepper
1 tsp. soy sauce

1 onion, sliced
1 green pepper, sliced
1 cup celery, chopped
1 can (16 oz.) stewed tomatoes
1 cup rice, cooked

Preheat oven to 350 degrees.
Using a non-stick cooking spray, grease a 2-qt. casserole dish.

In a skillet, brown meat with next 3 ingredients.

In baking dish, layer:
meat
onion
pepper
celery
tomatoes
rice

Bake (covered) 1 hour.

Serves 4.

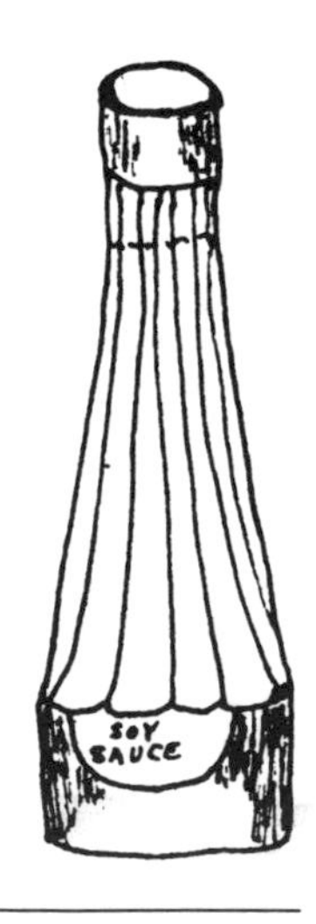

BEEF IN A BASKET

Our neighbors love this entree!

1 lb. ground round
1 onion, chopped
2 celery stalks, chopped
1 green pepper, chopped
1/2 cup picante sauce

1 can (10-ct.) biscuits

1/4 cup picante sauce
1 cup mozzarella cheese, shredded

Preheat oven to 400 degrees.
Using a non-stick cooking spray, grease a muffin pan.

In a skillet, brown first 5 ingredients.

Press biscuits into cups of the muffin pan.
Spoon meat mixture into all cups.
Top with picante sauce and cheese.

Bake 10-12 minutes.

Serves 5.

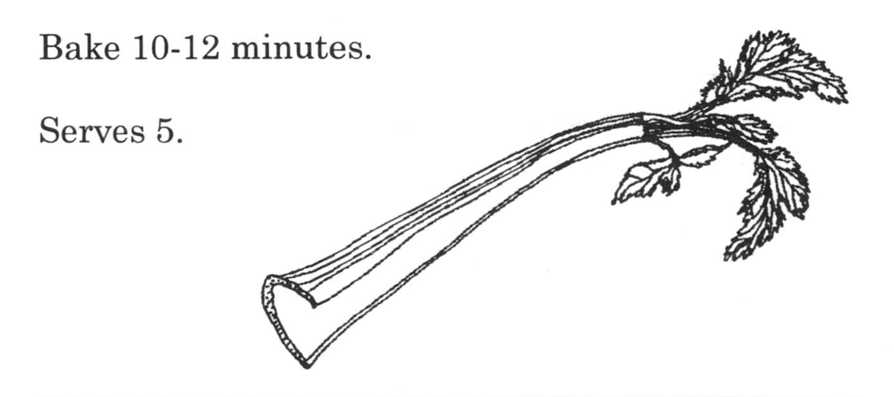

CHINCERITOS

A great Mexican flavor!

1½ lbs. ground round
2 onions, chopped

1 pkg. taco seasoning

1 pkg. (8-ct.) large flour tortillas

2 pkgs. (10 oz. size) Monterey Jack cheese with peppers, shredded
1 jar (16 oz.) salsa or picante sauce

2 cans (16 oz. size) chili with beans

Preheat oven to 350 degrees.
Using a non-stick cooking spray, grease two 9 x 13-inch baking dishes.

In a skillet, brown ground round and 1/2 of the onion. Set remaining onion aside.
Add taco seasoning and mix.

To assemble chinceritos:
Place meat (about 4 Tbsp.) on tortilla.
Sprinkle with onion, cheese, and salsa. (Save 1/2 cheese and salsa for topping.)
Fold tortilla over and place (seam down) in baking dish. (4 per dish)
Pour chili (directly from can) over center 2/3 of each tortilla.
Sprinkle with cheese.

Bake (uncovered) 30 minutes.
Spoon salsa over top just before serving.

Serves 8.

❤

GROUND ROUND PIE

This dish makes a good Sunday night supper.

1½ lbs. ground round
1/2 cup evaporated milk
1/2 cup corn flakes, crushed
1 onion, finely chopped
1/2 cup celery, finely chopped
1 tsp. Italian seasoning
1 tsp. black pepper
1/2 tsp. salt

2 frozen pie shells

1½ cups Monterey Jack cheese with peppers, shredded

Preheat oven to 350 degrees.

In a large bowl, combine first 8 ingredients.
Mix thoroughly.
Place 1/2 of mixture in each pie shell.
Bake 35 minutes.

Sprinkle tops with cheese.
Return to oven until cheese melts.

Serves 6-8.

MOCK POT PIE

1 lb. ground round
1 onion, chopped

1/2 cup frozen carrots, thawed
1/2 cup frozen broccoli, thawed

1 can (10¾ oz.) cream of chicken soup
1/2 soup can of milk

2 cans (8-ct.) crescent rolls
1 cup Monterey Jack cheese with peppers, shredded

Preheat oven to 375 degrees.
Using a non-stick cooking spray, lightly grease a large, shallow pan (15x10x1).

In a skillet, brown first 2 ingredients and drain.
Add next 2 ingredients. Cook 5 minutes.

Add next 2 ingredients. Heat thoroughly.

In a large, shallow pan, unroll 1 can of crescent rolls to form large rectangle. Press seams together.

On a piece of waxed paper, unroll second can of crescent rolls to form large rectangle. Press seams together.

Spoon meat mixture onto dough in pan.
Sprinkle cheese on top.
Lay second rectangle of dough over top. Gently peel off waxed paper. Press edges together to seal.

Bake (uncovered) 10-12 minutes.

Serves 6.

SWISS STEAK

salt
pepper
flour
2 lbs. round steak

3 Tbsp. cooking oil

1 can (16 oz.) stewed tomatoes
1 onion, sliced
2 celery stalks, chopped
1 green pepper, cut into strips
1 can (10 ¼ oz.) beef gravy

cooked rice

Preheat oven to 350 degrees.
Using a non-stick cooking spray, grease a shallow baking dish.

Sprinkle first 3 ingredients over steak and pound in.

In a skillet, brown steak in oil.

Place steak in baking dish.
Cover with next five ingredients.

Bake (covered) 1 hour or until tender.
Serve over rice.

Serves 6.

BEEF ROAST SIRIANO

Excellent when served over rice.

Marinade:
1/2 cup Italian salad dressing
1/4 tsp. garlic powder
1/2 tsp. oregano
1/4 tsp. thyme
1 tsp. cinnamon
1/2 cup sherry

1 boneless chuck roast (3-4 lbs.)

1 can (16 oz.) stewed tomatoes
3 green peppers, sliced
2 onions, sliced
salt

Mix marinade in a quart jar and shake vigorously.

Using a non-stick cooking spray, grease a large baking dish.
Place roast in dish and pour marinade over roast.
Cover and refrigerate (preferably overnight). Turn roast once in marinade

Preheat oven to 350 degrees.

Arrange next 3 ingredients over roast.
Sprinkle salt on top.
Spoon marinade over all.

Bake (covered) 2 hours or until tender.

Serves 6-8.

❤

CHUCK ROAST

2 envelopes Lipton onion soup
1 chuck roast (4 lbs.)

1 lb. carrots, sliced diagonally
1 lb. small potatoes, quartered
8 oz. fresh mushrooms, whole
1 bunch broccoli, cut into 2-inch pieces
1/2 cup water

Preheat oven to 350 degrees.
Using a non-stick cooking spray, grease a covered roasting pan.

Sprinkle 1 envelope of soup mix in bottom of pan.
Add roast.
Sprinkle 1 envelope of soup mix on roast.

Arrange vegetables around roast.
Add water.
Bake (covered) 2 hours.

Serves 8.

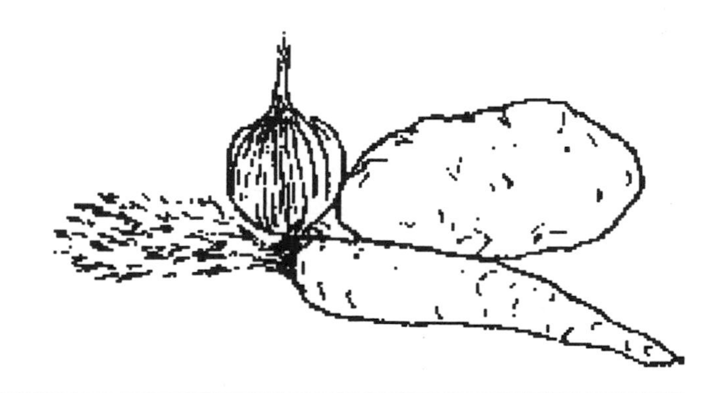

BEEF AU VIN

2 lbs. sirloin steak

1 can (10¾ oz.) French onion soup, undiluted
1 can (10¾ oz.) cream of mushroom soup, undiluted
1 cup red wine
1 tsp. black pepper
1/2 tsp. lemon pepper

1/4 cup cognac

parsley flakes

Preheat oven to 350 degrees.
Using a non-stick cooking spray, grease a large baking dish.

Place meat in dish.
Pour next 5 ingredients over meat.
Bake (covered) 2 hours.

Add cognac.
Bake (covered) 30 minutes.

Garnish with parsley flakes.

Serves 6.

PEPPER STEAK ORIENTALE

Garnish with Chinese noodles for a little crunch.

1 lb. sirloin steak, cut into thin strips
1/4 cup oil
1/2 tsp. salt
1/2 tsp. black pepper
1/2 tsp. lemon pepper

4 green peppers, cut into wedges
2 celery stalks, sliced
1 cup beef broth

1 tsp. cornstarch
1/4 cup water

2 tsp. soy sauce

Brown meat in oil and seasonings.

Add next 3 ingredients.
Cook (covered) until vegetables are tender.

Dissolve cornstarch in water.

Add soy sauce.
Mix thoroughly.
Add to meat mixture.
Cook (stirring constantly) until sauce thickens.

Serves 4.

SAUERBRATEN

2 lbs. sirloin steak, cut into bite-sized pieces
1/4 cup flour
1/2 stick of butter

1 onion, chopped
1 tsp. brown sugar
1 tsp. salt
1/2 tsp. ground ginger
1 tsp. Worcestershire sauce
2 bay leaves
2 Tbsp. wine vinegar
1/4 cup sherry
2 cups beef broth

1 can (10¾ oz.) cream of mushroom soup

6 cups cooked rice

Flour meat.
In a large Dutch oven, brown meat in butter.

Add next 9 ingredients.
Simmer (covered) 1 hour.

Remove bay leaves.
Add soup.
Heat thoroughly.

Serve over rice.

Serves 6-8.

STEAK CHARIVARI

Makes an elegant presentation.

1½ lbs. boneless sirloin (1/2-inch thick)

2 cups Pepperidge Farm herb seasoned stuffing mix

3 Tbsp. oil

2 cans (10¾ oz. size) cream of celery soup
2 soup cans milk

Pound steak to flatten.

Prepare stuffing mix according to package directions.
Spread stuffing mix over steak.
Roll steak and secure with string.

In a large skillet, brown steak roll in oil.

Blend soup with milk.
Pour over steak roll.
Simmer (covered) 1½ hours or until steak is tender (baste frequently).

Use soup mixture from pan as gravy when serving.

Serves 6.

FISH & SEAFOOD ENTREES

BAKED FLOUNDER

2 lbs. flounder fillets
minced garlic
black pepper

Italian salad dressing

Parmesan cheese

Preheat oven to 425 degrees.
Using a non-stick cooking spray, grease a large, shallow baking dish.

Rub seasonings on fish.
Place fish in baking dish.
Sprinkle salad dressing on fish.

Bake (uncovered) until fish flakes easily with a fork.

Sprinkle with Parmesan cheese and serve.

Serves 4.

TROUT ALMONDINE

Simple to prepare.

1 can (10¾ oz.) cream of celery soup
1/2 cup of milk

2 cups Pepperidge Farm herb seasoned stuffing mix

6 trout fillets

1 stick of butter
1 tsp. lemon pepper

1 cup slivered almonds

Preheat oven to 425 degrees.
Using a non-stick cooking spray, grease a large, shallow pan.

In a medium bowl, combine first 2 ingredients.

In a plastic bag, crush stuffing mix.

Dip trout into soup mixture.
Coat with stuffing mix.
Place on baking pan.
Bake (uncovered) 15 minutes.

Meanwhile:
On low heat, melt butter.
Add lemon pepper.

When trout is ready, sprinkle with almonds.
Pour butter over top and serve.

Serves 6.

FISH PARMESAN

1 lb. mild white fish fillets
1/4 tsp. seasoned salt
2 Tbsp. butter

1/2 cup grated Parmesan cheese
2 Tbsp. green onions, chopped
1/2 cup mayonnaise

paprika

Place fish on a platter.
Sprinkle with salt and dot with butter.
Cover with waxed paper.
Microwave on high 2 minutes.

In a small bowl, mix next 3 ingredients.
Spread over fish.
Microwave on high additional 2-3 minutes or until fish is flaky.

Sprinkle with paprika and serve.

Serves 4.

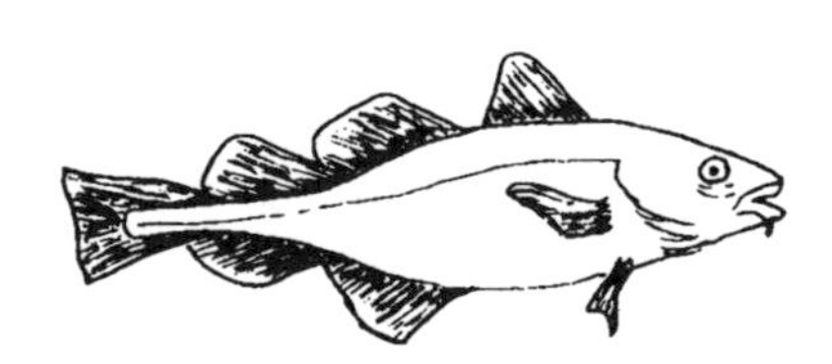

FISH PIQUANT

Spicy and good!

6 breaded fish fillets

2 cups Monterey Jack cheese with peppers, shredded
1/2 cup milk
1 tsp. chili powder
1/4 cup chili sauce
1/4 tsp. ground red pepper
dash of Tabasco

Preheat oven to 425 degrees.
Using a non-stick cooking spray, grease a 9 x 13-inch baking dish.

Place fish on baking dish.
Bake (uncovered) 20 minutes, turning once.

Meanwhile:
In a saucepan, combine remaining ingredients.

Cook (very low heat), stirring constantly, to form a smooth sauce.

Pour sauce over fish and serve immediately.

Serves 6.

BREAM OR CRAPPIE IN PUFFY BEER BATTER

You'll think you are in an English Pub!

6 medium bream or crappie, cleaned & dressed
lemon juice

1 cup all purpose flour
1 tsp. salt

1 cup all purpose flour
1 tsp. salt
1 Tbsp. paprika
1 can (12 oz.) beer

vegetable oil

lemon wedges

Dry fish.
Sprinkle both sides with lemon juice.
Set aside (best to refrigerate) for 15 minutes.

In a bowl, combine next 2 ingredients.

In a separate bowl, combine next 4 ingredients.
Mix thoroughly.

In a large Dutch oven, heat 1/2 inch oil to 360 degrees.

Dip fish in dry flour mixture.
Dip into beer/flour mixture.

Fry until golden brown.

Serves 6.

FESTIVE FISH FILLETS

This is a Florida fisherman's favorite recipe.

2 lbs. fish fillets, fresh or frozen

1/2 cup bottled French dressing

2 cups crushed cheese crackers

2 Tbsp. butter, melted
paprika

Preheat oven to 500 degrees.
Using a non-stick cooking spray, grease a cookie sheet.

Cut fillets into serving-size pieces.

Dip fish in dressing.

Roll in cracker crumbs.
Place on cookie sheet.

Drizzle butter over fish.
Sprinkle with paprika.

Bake 10-12 minutes (until fish flakes).

Serves 6.

CATFISH PARMESAN

2 lbs. frozen catfish, thawed

1 cup dry bread crumbs
3/4 cup grated Parmesan cheese
4 Tbsp. parsley flakes
1 tsp. paprika
1/2 tsp. oregano
2 tsp. salt
1 tsp. black pepper

1/2 cup butter, melted

lemon wedges

Preheat oven to 375 degrees.
Using a non-stick cooking spray, grease a 9 x 13-inch baking dish.

Wash and dry fish.

In a medium bowl, combine next 7 ingredients.
Mix.

Dip fish in butter.
Roll in crumb mixture.
Place in baking dish.

Drizzle butter over top.

Bake 25 minutes (until fish flakes).

Garnish with lemon wedges.

Serves 6.

SALMON CASSEROLE

2 eggs

1 can (16 oz.) cream style corn
1 can (16 oz.) salmon
1/2 tsp. black pepper
1 tsp. celery seed
1 can (10¾ oz.) cream of mushroom soup

1 cup Pepperidge Farm herb seasoned stuffing mix

Preheat oven to 350 degrees.
Using a non-stick cooking spray, grease a 1½-qt. casserole dish.

Break eggs into casserole dish.
Beat with a wire whisk.

Add next 5 ingredients.
Blend thoroughly

Sprinkle with stuffing mix.

Bake (uncovered) 30 minutes or until topping is browned.

Serves 6.

LEMON SHRIMP

Also makes a good appetizer.

2 lbs. medium shrimp, peeled

2 cloves garlic, halved
1/4 cup butter

3 Tbsp. lemon juice
1/2 tsp. salt
1 tsp. black pepper
3 drops Tabasco
1 Tbsp. Worcestershire sauce

3 Tbsp. fresh parsley, chopped

Preheat broiler.
Using a non-stick cooking spray, grease a jelly roll pan (15 x10 x1).
Place shrimp (single layer) on pan.

In a skillet, saute garlic in butter.
Discard garlic.

Add next 5 ingredients.
Mix thoroughly.
Pour over shrimp.

Broil 4 inches from heat, 8-10 minutes. Baste once.
Sprinkle with parsley and serve.

Serves 6.

❤

RIVERCHASE SHRIMP

A tasty dish from Mississippi.

2 cups cooked shrimp, chopped
1/2 cup onions, diced
1/2 cup pimento, diced
1 cup celery, diced
1 cup sharp cheddar cheese, cubed
1 can (8 oz.) sliced water chestnuts
1/2 cup sliced almonds
3/4 cup mayonnaise

2 cups Ritz cracker crumbs

Preheat oven to 350 degrees.
Using a non-stick cooking spray, grease a 2-qt. baking dish.

In large mixing bowl, combine first 8 ingredients.
Mix thoroughly.
Turn into baking dish.

Top with cracker crumbs.

Bake (uncovered) 30-45 minutes.

Serves 8.

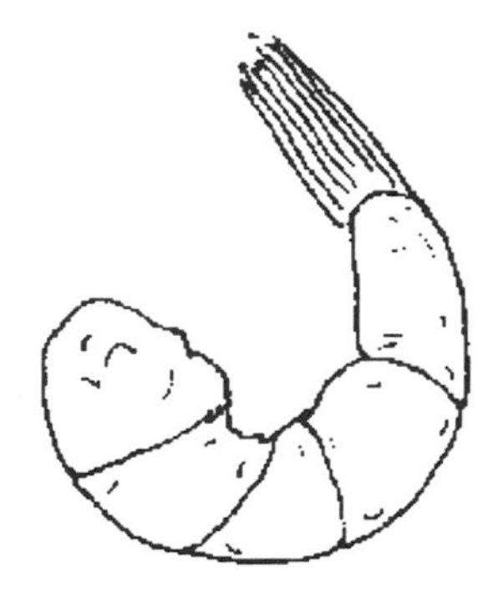

The Lazy Cook–type shrimp—peeled, cooked, and ready for the hor d'oeuvre platter. Remove tails before adding to recipes.

SHRIMP CHARLESTONIAN

2 lbs. fresh or frozen shrimp

4 cups cooked rice
1 pint cream
1 cup milk
1 tsp. salt
1/4 tsp. pepper
1/4 tsp. Tabasco
1 Tbsp. Worcestershire sauce
5 Tbsp. catsup
1 green pepper, chopped
1/4 cup sherry

Boil shrimp 3-4 minutes (until pink).

Preheat oven to 400 degrees.
Using a non-stick cooking spray, grease a 9 x 13-inch casserole.

Clean shrimp. Chop into small pieces.

Combine shrimp with remaining ingredients.
Turn into casserole dish.

Bake (uncovered) 15-20 minutes.

Serves 6.

Lazy Cook's least favorite way to get shrimp—live!

SHRIMP CREOLE

1 onion, chopped
2 celery stalks, chopped
1 green pepper, chopped
1/2 cup olive oil
1 tsp. minced garlic

1 can (16 oz.) stewed tomatoes
2 cups chicken broth
1 cup Rhine wine
1 cup milk

1 pkg. (6 oz.) Uncle Ben's long grain & wild rice mix, uncooked

1 lb. frozen shrimp, thawed

Parmesan cheese

In a large Dutch oven, saute first 3 ingredients in oil and garlic.

Add next 4 ingredients.
Simmer (covered) 10 minutes.

Add rice.
Simmer (covered) 25 minutes.

Add shrimp.
Heat thoroughly.
Sprinkle with Parmesan cheese and serve.

Serves 6.

❤

SHRIMP EN APRE CREME

Literally translates: Shrimp in Sour Cream Sauce.

2 lbs. fresh or frozen shrimp, peeled and cleaned
1 small onion, minced
1/2 cup butter

1 lb. fresh mushrooms, sliced

2 Tbsp. flour
1 tsp. salt
1 tsp. black pepper

3 cups sour cream

1/4 cup cooking sherry

cooked rice

In a heavy saucepan, saute first 2 ingredients in butter.
Cook 5 minutes or until shrimp is pink.

Add mushrooms.
Cook 5 minutes (stirring frequently).

Blend in next 3 ingredients.

Gradually stir in sour cream.

Cook over low heat (stirring constantly) until mixture is thick.
Remove from heat.
Stir in sherry.

Serve over rice.

Serves 6.

SHRIMP GUMBO

1 can (16 oz.) stewed tomatoes
8 oz. frozen okra, thawed
(microwave on high 2 minutes)
1/2 tsp. minced garlic
1/2 tsp. lemon pepper
1/4 tsp. ground red pepper

1 lb. frozen shrimp, thawed

4 cups cooked rice

In a large saucepan, bring to a boil the first 5 ingredients.
Reduce heat and simmer (covered) 5 minutes.

Add shrimp.
Simmer (covered) 10 minutes.

Serve over rice.

Serves 4.

CAJUN OYSTERS

New Orleans style!

4 Tbsp. butter
2 pts. oysters, drained

1/4 cup dry white wine
2 Tbsp. lemon juice
2 tsp. Worcestershire sauce
1 tsp. salt
1/2 tsp. Tabasco

toast points

In a large skillet, melt butter (low heat).
Add oysters.
Cook until edges curl (about 5 minutes).

Add next 5 ingredients.
Heat thoroughly.

Serve over toast points.

Serves 6.

OYSTER SCALLOP

1 pt. oysters

2 cups cracker crumbs
1/2 tsp. salt
1/2 tsp. black pepper
1/2 cup butter

1/4 tsp. Worcestershire sauce
1/2 cup milk

Preheat oven to 350 degrees.
Using a non-stick cooking spray, grease a 1½-qt. casserole dish.

Drain oysters. Set aside.

In a bowl, combine next 4 ingredients.
Sprinkle 1/3 of mixture in casserole dish.
Cover with 1/2 of oysters.
Repeat layers.

Combine next 2 ingredients.
Pour over casserole.
Top with remaining crumb mixture.

Bake (uncovered) 30 minutes or until brown.

Serves 4.

CRAB DE LA CREME

2 Tbsp. butter
2 Tbsp. flour
1 cup milk

1/4 cup sherry
1/4 tsp. salt
3/4 tsp. pepper
1/2 tsp. basil
1/2 tsp. chives
1/2 tsp. dried onions
1/2 tsp. Creole seasoning
1/4 tsp. seasoned salt
1/2 tsp. Tabasco

1/2 lb. crabmeat

In a large saucepan, melt butter.
Stir in flour.
Add milk slowly.
Cook (stirring constantly) until thickened.

Fold in next 9 ingredients.

Add crabmeat.
Simmer an additional 2 minutes.

Serve over toast points.

Serves 4.

❤

CRABMEAT QUICHE

1 frozen pie shell

3 eggs, slightly beaten
1 cup sour cream
1/2 tsp. Worcestershire sauce
3/4 tsp. salt

1 cup Swiss cheese, shredded
1 can (6½ oz.) crabmeat, drained and flaked
1 can (3½ oz.) French fried onions

Preheat oven to 400 degrees.
Partially bake pie shell (about 5 minutes).

Reduce oven temperature to 350 degrees.

In a large mixing bowl, combine the next 4 ingredients. Mix thoroughly.

Stir in the next 3 ingredients.
Pour into baked pie shell.

Bake (uncovered) 30-40 minutes (until knife inserted in center comes out clean).

Serves 6.

CRAB ROYALE

2 cups cooked crabmeat, drained and flaked
1 cup shredded cheddar cheese
1/3 cup Pepperidge Farm herb seasoned stuffing mix
1/2 cup chopped celery
1/2 cup mayonnaise
1/3 cup milk
3 Tbsp. chopped green pepper
2 tsp. minced onion
2 tsp. lemon juice
salt
black pepper
lemon pepper
ground red pepper

Preheat oven to 375 degrees.
Using a non-stick cooking spray, grease 6 ramekins or a small baking dish.,

In a mixing bowl, combine all ingredients.
Mix thoroughly.

Turn into ramekins.

Bake (uncovered) 15 minutes (lightly browned).

Serves 6.

JAMBALAYA

A favorite in the South.

6 slices bacon, chopped

1 medium onion, chopped
1 celery stalk, chopped
1 small green pepper, chopped

1 can (28 oz.) tomatoes, undrained and chopped
1/4 cup long grain white rice, uncooked
1 Tbsp. Worcestershire sauce
1/2 tsp. salt
1/2 tsp. black pepper

2 cans (6 oz. size) crabmeat, drained and flaked

In a large skillet, cook bacon.
Add next 3 ingredients.
Cook until tender.

Add next 5 ingredients.
Cover and simmer 25 minutes (until rice is tender).

Add crabmeat.
Heat thoroughly.

Serves 4.

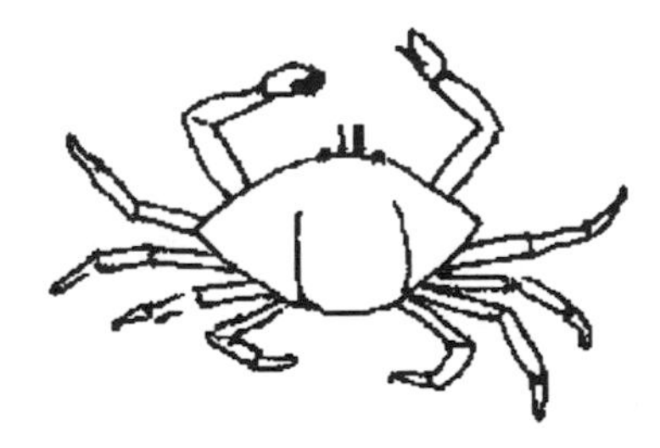

PORK ENTREES

APPLE-STUFFED PORK TENDERLOINS

Even William Tell could not have resisted this dish!

2 cups apple juice
1 Tbsp. butter

3/4 cup apple, diced
1/2 cup onion, diced
3/4 cup Pepperidge Farm herb seasoned stuffing mix

2 whole pork tenderloins (1 lb. each)
salt
pepper

4 slices bacon, cut in half

Preheat oven to 350 degrees.
Using a non-stick cooking spray, grease a large, shallow baking dish.

In a saucepan, combine:
1/2 cup apple juice (save remaining juice)
butter

Heat, stirring constantly, until butter melts.

Add next 3 ingredients.
Blend thoroughly.

Cut tenderloins lengthwise (but not all the way through) and flatten.
Place one in baking dish.
Sprinkle with salt and pepper.
Spread stuffing mixture on top.
Place second tenderloin over stuffing and skewer shut.

Arrange bacon on top.
Pour reserved apple juice over meat. Baste frequently with juice.
Bake (uncovered) 1½ hrs. (Let stand 5 minutes before slicing.)

Serves 6.

CREOLE PORK

2 Tbsp. vegetable oil
4 pork steaks

1 stalk celery, chopped
1 can (16 oz.) tomato sauce
1 cup water
1/2 cup milk
2 Tbsp. brown sugar
1 tsp. salt
1/4 tsp. basil
1 cup uncooked long grain white rice

In a large skillet, brown pork steak in oil.
Drain excess fat.

Add remaining ingredients.
Cover and simmer 30 minutes (until steaks and rice are tender).

Serves 4.

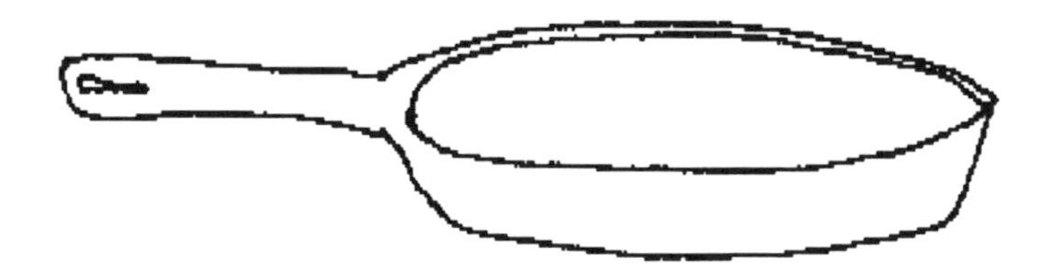

PORK ROAST A LA ORANGE

Serve with a salad, Rice Spice (p. 105), and Carrots a la Yum (p. 101).

1 pork roast (3 lbs.)
1/4 tsp. salt
1 tsp. black pepper
1 tsp. lemon pepper
1/4 tsp. allspice

1/2 cup water
1/2 cup Karo syrup
1 cup orange juice concentrate

cinnamon

Preheat oven to 350 degrees.
Using a non-stick cooking spray, grease a large roasting pan and rack.

Place roast on rack.
Sprinkle with seasonings.

Combine next 3 ingredients.
Pour over roast.

Roast (uncovered) 2 hours. Baste frequently.
When no longer pink in center (185° F.), sprinkle with cinnamon and serve.

Serves 6-8.

❤

FRUITY PORK CHOPS

6 pork chops (1-inch thick)
salt
pepper
minced garlic

6 onion slices
6 orange slices
6 apple rings

brown sugar

Preheat oven to 350 degrees.
Using a non-stick cooking spray, grease a large, shallow baking dish.

Arrange pork chops in dish.
Sprinkle with seasonings.

Add 1 slice of next 3 ingredients to each pork chop.

Sprinkle with brown sugar.

Bake (covered) 45 minutes.
Uncover and bake until browned.

Serves 6.

PORK CHOPS AND SPANISH RICE

4 pork chops
3 Tbsp. oil

1 onion, chopped
1 green pepper, chopped

1 can (16 oz.) stewed tomatoes
1/2 cup sherry
1 Tbsp. flour
2 Tbsp. lemon juice
1 tsp. minced garlic
1/2 cup rice, half-cooked

3/4 cup hot water
2 chicken bouillon cubes

Using a non-stick cooking spray, grease a 9 x 13-inch casserole dish.
Preheat oven to 350 degrees.

In a skillet, brown pork chops in oil.
Remove to casserole dish.

Saute next two ingredients in remaining oil.
Add to dish.

Add next 6 ingredients to dish.

Dissolve bouillon in water.
Pour over casserole.

Bake (covered) 20 minutes.
Remove cover and bake additional 10 minutes.

Serves 4.

SWISS PORK CHOPS

6 pork chops
salt
pepper
prepared mustard

flour
2 Tbsp. butter

1 can (10¾ oz.) cream of chicken soup
1/2 soup can of milk

1 onion, chopped

1 cup Swiss cheese, shredded

Rub seasonings on pork chops.
Spread mustard on each.

Dip in flour.
In a large covered skillet, brown in butter.
Drain excess fat from pan.

Mix next 2 ingredients.
Pour over pork chops.
Add onion.
Simmer (covered) 30 minutes.

Sprinkle cheese over top.
Simmer until cheese melts.

Serves 6.

❤

BAKED HAM SLICES

2 center slices of ham

2 tsp. prepared mustard
4 Tbsp. brown sugar

milk

Preheat oven to 325 degrees.
Using a non-stick cooking spray, grease a large baking dish.

Score ham slices to prevent curling.

Spread each top with mustard.
Sprinkle with brown sugar.
Place flat in dish.

Add milk to dish until even with top of ham. Do not cover ham with milk!

Bake (uncovered) 40 minutes.

Turn ham.
Spread with mustard.
Sprinkle with brown sugar.

Bake (uncovered) additional 35 minutes. (Milk should be absorbed and ham golden brown.)

Serves 4.

❤

HAM ROLLS

Can also be made with asparagus.

2 pkgs. (10 oz. size) frozen broccoli spears

12 slices (6-8 in. long) Danish ham
12 slices (6-8 in. long) Swiss cheese

1 can (10¾ oz.) cream of mushroom soup
1/2 soup can of milk
1 can (4 oz.) mushroom pieces
1/4 tsp. lemon pepper
1/2 tsp. black pepper

paprika

Preheat oven to 350 degrees.
Using a non-stick cooking spray, grease a 9 x 13-inch baking dish.

Cook broccoli according to package directions.
Place cheese on top of ham and roll around each broccoli stalk.
Arrange in baking dish.

Combine next 5 ingredients.
Pour soup mixture over ham rolls.
Sprinkle with paprika.

Bake (uncovered) 30 minutes.

Serves 6.

HAM WITH APRICOT SAUCE

2 lb. boneless cooked ham slice, cut into 6 pieces
2 Tbsp. vegetable oil

1 onion, sliced

1 can (12 oz.) apricot nectar

2 tsp. cornstarch
1/4 cup cold water

In a large skillet, brown ham in oil.
Remove from skillet.

Add onion.
Cook (medium heat) until tender.

Stir in apricot nectar.
Return ham to skillet.
Cover and simmer 15 minutes (basting frequently).
Remove ham to serving platter.

Dissolve cornstarch in cold water.
Add to skillet.
Cook (stirring constantly) until thickened.
Pour over ham.

Serves 6.

COUNTRY BARBECUE

3 lbs. country-style ribs
2 onions, sliced
lemon juice

1 Tbsp. paprika
1 tsp. ground mustard
1 tsp. ground red pepper
1/2 tsp. salt
1 tsp. chili powder
2 Tbsp. sugar
1/4 cup vinegar
1/4 cup water
1 cup tomato juice
2 Tbsp. Worcestershire sauce
1/4 cup catsup

Preheat oven to 400 degrees.
Using a non-stick cooking spray, grease a large, shallow baking dish.

Arrange ribs in baking dish.
Place onion slices over ribs.
Sprinkle with lemon juice.
Bake (uncovered) 30 min.

<u>Meanwhile</u>:
In a saucepan, combine remaining ingredients.
Simmer (stir frequently) until slightly thickened.

Reduce oven temperature to 250 degrees.
Pour sauce over ribs.
Bake (uncovered) 2½ hours.

Serves 6.

QUICHE LORRAINE

1 frozen pie shell
6 oz. Swiss cheese
8 oz. bacon, cooked and broken into pieces
1 green pepper, chopped
1/2 cup green onion, chopped
1 can (4 oz.) mushrooms

3 eggs
1½ cups heavy cream

1 tsp. flour
1/2 tsp. salt
1/2 tsp. black pepper

Preheat oven to 400 degrees.

Partially bake pie shell (about 5 minutes).

Reduce oven to 350 degrees.

Arrange next 5 ingredients in pie shell.

Beat eggs and cream together.

Add next 3 ingredients.
Pour egg mixture over pie shell.

Bake (uncovered) 30-40 minutes.

Serves 6.

BRATS 'N' BEER

Krystyn's favorite meal!

2 qts. beer
1 tsp. minced garlic
1 tsp. black pepper

2 lbs. bratwurst

2 cans (16 oz. size) sauerkraut

In a large stockpot, bring beer and seasonings to a boil.

Add bratwurst.
Reduce heat and simmer (uncovered) 30 minutes.

Remove sausages and brown on a grill (charcoal provides best flavor).

Serve with sauerkraut.

Serves 6.

KIELBASA UND KOHL

This dish would be complemented with fresh apple slices.

1 lb. kielbasa (Polish sausage), sliced into bite-sized pieces

2 cups cabbage, shredded
2 cups potatoes, sliced, unpeeled
1 onion, chopped
1 cup water
1 tsp. black pepper
1 tsp. horseradish sauce

In a large skillet, brown kielbasa.

Add remaining ingredients.
Cook (covered) over medium heat until potatoes are tender.

Serves 6.

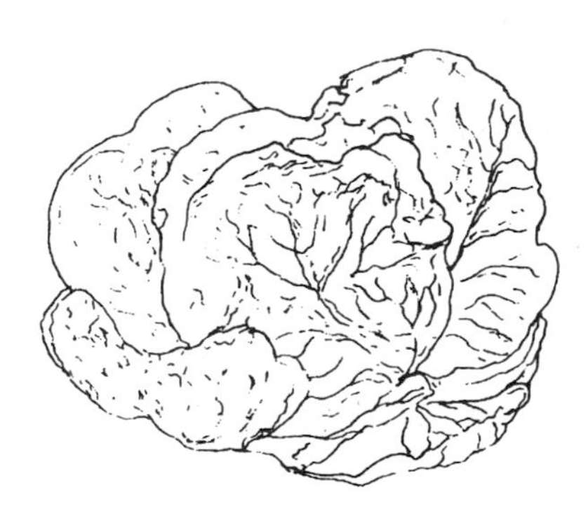

MEXICAN SAUSAGE CASSEROLE

2 lbs. pork sausage
1 onion, chopped
1 green pepper, chopped
1/2 tsp. minced garlic

2 cans (16 oz. size) stewed tomatoes
2 cups buttermilk
2 cups macaroni, uncooked
1 Tbsp. sugar
2 tsp. chili powder
1 tsp. salt
1 tsp. black pepper

In a large skillet, brown first 4 ingredients.
Drain.

Add remaining ingredients.
Mix thoroughly.
Cover.
Simmer 10-15 minutes or until macaroni is cooked.

Serves 6.

PASTA FIGIOLI

1 lb. pork sausage
1 onion, diced
1 green pepper, diced
1 tsp. minced garlic

1 can (16 oz.) tomatoes
1 cup buttermilk
1 cup macaroni, uncooked
1 can (16 oz.) kidney beans, undrained
2 tsp. sugar
2 tsp. chili powder
1/4 tsp. crushed red pepper
1 tsp. Italian seasoning

In a large skillet, cook (medium heat) the first 4 ingredients. Drain.

Add remaining ingredients.
Mix thoroughly.
Cover and cook on high until steaming.
Reduce heat and simmer 10-15 minutes (until macaroni is soft).

Serves 6.

PICADIA

Even if you aren't Spanish, you'll love this dish.

1 onion, chopped
1 green pepper, chopped
1 Tbsp. butter

1 lb. pork sausage
1 lb. ground chuck
1 tsp. minced garlic

1 can (16 oz.) whole tomatoes
3 bay leaves
1 cup green olives with pimentos, chopped
1 cup raisins

2 pkgs. (5 oz.) yellow rice

1 can (16 oz.) green peas

In a heavy Dutch oven, saute first 2 ingredients in butter.

Add next 3 ingredients and brown.

Add next 4 ingredients.
Simmer (covered) 1 hour.

Cook rice according to package directions.

Heat peas in saucepan and drain.

Spread rice on large platter.
Pour meat mixture over rice. Remove bay leaves.
Top with green peas.

Serves 6.

SAUSAGE CASSEROLE

Makes a nice breakfast for guests.

1/2 lb. bulk sausage

2 cups cheddar cheese, shredded

2 eggs
1 cup Bisquick
1 cup milk

Preheat oven to 350 degrees.
Using a non-stick cooking spray, grease a 9 x 9-inch baking dish.

Cook sausage.
Drain and set aside.

Place cheese in baking dish.
Sprinkle sausage over it.

In a medium bowl, combine next 3 ingredients.
Pour over sausage mixture.

Bake (uncovered) 45-50 minutes or until golden brown.

Serves 4.

STUFFED ACORN SQUASH

3 acorn squash

1/3 cup molasses
1 tsp. salt
1 tsp. black pepper

1 lb. bulk pork sausage
bread crumbs

Preheat oven to 400 degrees.

Wash squash.
Cut in halves and remove seeds.

Put a tablespoon of molasses in each half.
Sprinkle with salt and pepper.

Fill each squash with sausage.
Sprinkle with bread crumbs.

Place in baking pan with 1 inch of water.

Bake (covered) 40 minutes.
Remove cover and brown.

Serves 6.

POULTRY ENTREES

APRICOT CHICKEN

6 boneless chicken breasts
salt
pepper

1 can (21 oz.) apricot pie filling*
1 Tbsp. lemon juice
1/2 tsp. salt
1/2 tsp. ground nutmeg
1/2 cup pecan halves

cooked rice

Preheat oven to 350 degrees.
Using a non-stick cooking spray, grease a 9 x 13-inch baking dish.
Arrange chicken (single layer) in dish.
Sprinkle with salt and pepper.

In a mixing bowl, combine next 5 ingredients.
Mix thoroughly.
Pour over chicken.
Bake (covered) 40 minutes.

Serve over hot rice.

Serves 6.

**Apricot preserves or "all-fruit" preserves may be substituted. To do so, bake chicken (covered) 25 minutes. In a saucepan, heat ingredients 4-8. Pour over chicken and bake (covered) an additional 15 minutes.*

CHICKEN DIJON

4 boneless chicken breasts
1/2 cup flour
3 Tbsp. butter

2 Tbsp. flour

1 cup chicken broth
1/2 cup light cream

1 Tbsp. Dijon mustard

2 tomatoes, cut into wedges
parsley

Coat chicken breasts with flour.
In a large covered skillet, cook in butter until tender and browned (about 20 minutes).

Remove chicken from pan.
Brown flour in pan drippings.

Add next 2 ingredients.
Cook (stirring constantly) until thickened.

Stir in mustard.

Return chicken to pan.
Cook (covered) 10 minutes.

Garnish with tomato and parsley.

Serves 4.

CHICKEN MALDEN

Good "company food."

6 boneless chicken breasts
6 slices bacon

12 oz. fresh mushrooms, whole

1 can (10¾ oz.) cream of mushroom soup
1 cup sour cream
1/2 cup half & half
1 jar (2 oz.) pimentos
1 tsp. black pepper
1 tsp. minced garlic
1/2 tsp. onion powder

Preheat oven to 300 degrees.
Using a non-stick cooking spray, grease a large, shallow baking dish.

Wrap each chicken breast with bacon.
Place in baking dish.
Arrange mushrooms in dish.

In a large bowl, combine remaining ingredients.
Pour over chicken.

Bake (covered) 1 hour or until chicken is tender. (Baste occasionally.)

Serves 6.

CHICKEN MANTELLO

Translated literally means "chicken in a wrap."

3 potatoes, sliced
2 zucchini, sliced
6 chicken breasts, brushed with oil
1/4 cup Italian salad dressing
black pepper
Italian seasoning
8 oz. mushrooms, sliced
6 Tbsp. butter

Preheat oven to 400 degrees.

Cut six pieces of aluminum foil.
On each, layer:
potato slices
zucchini slices
chicken breast
salad dressing
black pepper
Italian seasoning
mushrooms
1 Tbsp. butter

Wrap each tightly.
Bake on a cookie sheet 1 hour.

Serves 6.

CHICKEN MOUTARDE

2 cups water

1 whole chicken (2-3 lbs.)

1 tsp. salt
1 tsp. black pepper
1 tsp. lemon pepper
1 Tbsp. minced garlic
1 tsp. ground mustard

1/4 cup horseradish mustard
1 can (10¾ oz.) cream of chicken soup
1/2 soup can milk
1 cup Monterey Jack cheese with peppers, shredded

Preheat oven to 350 degrees.
Using a non-stick cooking spray, grease a large roasting pan with rack.

Place water in roasting pan.
Clean chicken and place on rack in pan.
Sprinkle with seasonings.
Bake (uncovered) 1½ hrs. (Leg should pull easily when thoroughly cooked.)

Meanwhile:
In a saucepan combine remaining ingredients.
Cook over low heat, stirring constantly, to form smooth sauce.

When chicken is ready, pour sauce over it and bake (basting frequently) an additional 10 minutes.

Serves 4-6.

CHICKEN NOTORIO

Tasty and quick.

6 boneless chicken breasts

1 can (10¾ oz.) cream of celery soup
1 cup sour cream
3/4 cup sherry
1 can (4 oz.) mushrooms
1 jar (2 oz.) pimentos
1 tsp. black pepper
1 tsp. lemon pepper

chives

Preheat oven to 350 degrees.
Using a non-stick cooking spray, grease a 9 x 13-inch baking dish.

Place chicken in baking dish.

In a bowl, combine next 7 ingredients.
Mix thoroughly with a wire whisk.
Pour over chicken.

Sprinkle with chives.

Bake (covered) 40 minutes.

Serves 6.

❤

CHICKEN PIE

A good use for leftover chicken or turkey.

1 onion, chopped
2 Tbsp. butter

2 Tbsp. all purpose flour

1 can (10¾ oz.) chicken noodle soup, undiluted
1 can (10¾ oz.) cream of chicken soup, undil.

2 cups cooked chicken, chopped
1/2 tsp. salt
1 tsp. black pepper

1 can (10-ct.) biscuits
Parmesan cheese

Preheat oven to 400 degrees.
Using a non-stick cooking spray, grease a 2-qt. casserole dish.

In a large saucepan, saute onion in butter.

Blend in flour.

Add next 2 ingredients.
Heat until thickened.

Add next 3 ingredients.
Heat thoroughly.

Pour into casserole dish.
Arrange biscuits on top.
Sprinkle with Parmesan cheese.

Bake (uncovered) 10-12 min. (until biscuits brown).

Serves 5.

CHICKEN AND RICE

Makes a good "covered dish."

1¼ cups rice, uncooked

1 can (10¾ oz.) cream of mushroom soup
1 can (10¾ oz.) cream of celery soup
1 can (10¾ oz.) cream of chicken soup
1 soup can milk
1/4 cup butter, melted
1/4 cup dry sherry
1/2 tsp. black pepper
1 tsp. celery seed
1 tsp. ground red pepper

10 chicken pieces

slivered almonds
fresh Parmesan cheese, shredded

Preheat oven to 325 degrees.
Using a non-stick cooking spray, grease a shallow 3-qt. baking dish.

Sprinkle rice on bottom of dish.

In a large bowl, combine next 9 ingredients.
Blend thoroughly with a wire whisk.
Spread 1/2 of soup mixture over rice.

Arrange chicken pieces over soup.
Spread remaining soup mixture over chicken.

Sprinkle with almonds and cheese.
Bake covered 1½ hours or until chicken is tender.

Serves 6-8.

♥

CHICKEN STUFFED INSIDE-OUT

You will receive many compliments on this dish.

1 pkg. (8 oz.) Pepperidge Farm herb seasoned stuffing mix
1/4 cup butter, melted

1 can (10¾ oz.) cream of chicken soup
1/3 cup milk

8 boneless chicken breasts

Preheat oven to 375 degrees.
Using a non-stick cooking spray, grease a large cookie sheet.

In a large bowl, combine first 2 ingredients.
Mix well.

In a medium bowl, combine next 2 ingredients.
Blend thoroughly.

Dip 1 piece of chicken into soup mix.
Then into stuffing. Press mixture on. (If mixture is too dry, add water.)
Place on cookie sheet.
Repeat with each piece.

Bake 45 minutes - 1 hour.

Serves 8.

❤

CHICKEN STIR FRY

1/4 cup peanut oil
2 tsp. minced garlic
1 tsp. lemon pepper

1 lb. boneless chicken breasts, cut into bite-sized pieces

1 onion, chopped

2 cups chicken broth
1/2 tsp. salt

1 cup frozen carrots, thawed
1 cup frozen broccoli, thawed
1 can (8 oz.) sliced water chestnuts, drained
1 can (8 oz.) bamboo shoots, drained

2 Tbsp. cornstarch
1/4 cup cold water
1 Tbsp. soy sauce

6 cups cooked rice

Heat oil and seasonings on medium high in a large wok or skillet.

Add chicken and cook 2 minutes.

Add onion and cook an additional 3 minutes.

❤

Add next 2 ingredients and bring to a boil.

Add next 4 ingredients and return to a boil.
Reduce heat and cook (covered) 3 minutes or until vegetables are tender.

Dissolve cornstarch in water, then stir in soy sauce.
Pour slowly into wok, stirring constantly.
Cook until thickened (about 3 minutes).
Serve over rice.

Serves 6.

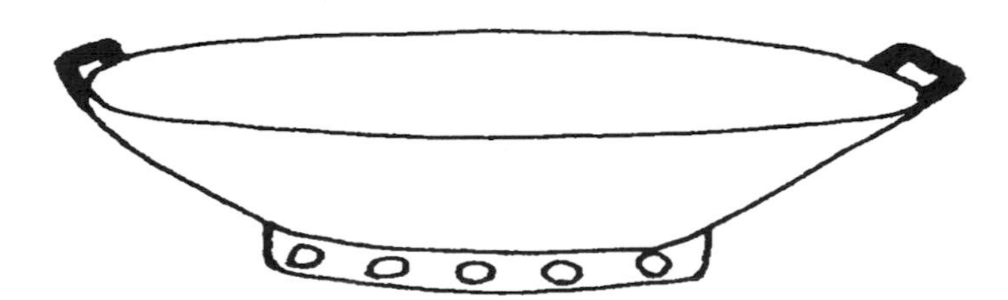

HAWAIIAN CHICKEN

6 boneless chicken breasts
1/2 cup butter, melted

black pepper

1 cup orange juice
2 Tbsp. lemon juice
1/2 cup brown sugar
1 Tbsp. soy sauce
2 Tbsp. cornstarch

1 can (16 oz.) pineapple slices

Preheat oven to 350 degrees.
Using a non-stick cooking spray, grease a 9 x 13-inch baking dish.

Saute chicken in 1/2 of the butter.
Place chicken in baking dish.
Brush with remaining butter.

Sprinkle with pepper.
Bake (uncovered) 20 minutes.

Meanwhile:
Combine next 5 ingredients in a saucepan.
Cook over medium heat (stirring constantly) until thickened.

Pour sauce over chicken.
Top with pineapple slices.
Bake (uncovered) 15 minutes.

Serves 6.

HONG KONG CHICKEN

1/4 cup soy sauce
1 tsp. salt
1 tsp. cornstarch
1/2 tsp. garlic powder
1 Tbsp. sugar
1/4 tsp. ground ginger
1 tsp. black pepper

6 boneless chicken breasts, in 1/2-inch pieces
2 Tbsp. vegetable oil

1/3 cup vegetable oil
2 green peppers, chopped into 1/2-inch pieces
1 can (8 oz.) bamboo shoots, drained

2 Tbsp. honey
1/2 cup cashew nuts

chow mein noodles

In a mixing bowl, combine first 7 ingredients. (Set aside 2 Tbsp. of mixture.)
Add chicken and toss to coat.

In a large skillet, heat 2 Tbsp. of vegetable oil.
Cook chicken in oil (5-7 minutes) then remove.

Add next 3 ingredients and reserved soy sauce mixture to skillet.
Cook 3-4 minutes.

Return chicken to skillet and stir gently.
Stir in honey and cook 3 minutes.
Remove from heat and add cashews.

Serve over chow mein noodles.

Serves 6.

ORIENTAL CHICKEN

4 boneless chicken breasts
salt
pepper

2 cups celery, chopped
1 medium onion, chopped
1 can (8 oz.) sliced water chestnuts, drained

1/2 cup mayonnaise
1 can (10¾ oz.) cream of chicken soup

paprika

Preheat oven to 350 degrees.
Using a non-stick cooking spray, grease a 9 x 13-inch baking dish.

Place chicken in dish.
Sprinkle with salt and pepper.

Arrange next 3 ingredients in dish.

In a small bowl, combine soup and mayonnaise.
Mix thoroughly.
Pour over chicken.

Sprinkle with paprika.

Bake (covered) 45 minutes.
Remove cover and brown.

Serves 4.

OVEN-FRIED CHICKEN

You'll never use the skillet again.

1 cup Bisquick
1 tsp. paprika
1 tsp. poultry seasoning
1 tsp. salt

1 can (5 oz.) evaporated milk

4 boneless chicken breasts

4 Tbsp. butter, melted

Preheat oven to 375 degrees.
Using a non-stick cooking spray, grease a 9 x 13-inch baking dish.

In a medium mixing bowl, combine first 4 ingredients. Mix thoroughly.

Pour milk into a second bowl.

Dip chicken pieces in milk, then coat with dry ingredients.
Place in baking dish.

Drizzle melted butter over chicken.

Bake (uncovered) 45 minutes - 1 hour.

Serves 4.

CHICKEN L'ORANGE

This dish makes an elegant presentation.

1 can (6 oz.) orange juice concentrate

1/2 stick butter

1 chicken, quartered
salt
pepper

Preheat oven to 300 degrees.
Using a non-stick cooking spray, grease a large baking dish.

Thaw orange juice concentrate and set aside.

Melt butter and set aside.

Place chicken in baking dish.
Sprinkle chicken with salt and pepper.

Pour butter over chicken.

Pour orange juice concentrate over chicken.

Bake (uncovered) 1 hour or until chicken is tender.

Serves 4.

CHICKEN CRISP

1 chicken, cut into pieces

1/2 cup sour cream
1 Tbsp. lemon juice
1 tsp. Worcestershire sauce
1 tsp. celery salt
1/2 tsp. paprika
2 tsp. granulated garlic
1 tsp. salt
1 tsp. black pepper

bread or cracker crumbs

Preheat oven to 350 degrees.
Grease a large baking dish.

Rinse chicken, pat dry.

Combine next 8 ingredients.

Dip chicken in cream mixture.
Roll chicken in crumbs.
Place chicken in baking dish.

Bake (uncovered) 1 hour.

Serves 4.

CHICKEN PENTOLA

1 can (16 oz.) stewed tomatoes
2 onions, chopped
2 green peppers, chopped
6 potatoes, sliced
1 can (6 oz.) mushrooms
1 pkg. (3 oz.) slivered almonds
1 cup raisins
1 Tbsp. olive oil
1 cup black olives, sliced
1 cup Rhine wine
2 lbs. chicken, cut into pieces
1 tsp. black pepper
1 tsp. granulated garlic
1 tsp. lemon pepper
1/2 tsp. ground red pepper

Place all ingredients in a large Dutch oven.
Cook (covered) over medium heat until chicken is tender (1 hour).

Serves 6.

TURKEY ALMONDINE

3 cups cooked turkey, cubed
1 can (10¾ oz.) cream of chicken soup
1 can (8 oz.) sliced water chestnuts, undrained
1 can (4 oz.) sliced mushrooms, undrained
2/3 cup mayonnaise
1/2 cup chopped celery
2 Tbsp. minced onion
1/2 cup sour cream

1 can (8-ct.) crescent rolls

2/3 cup shredded Swiss cheese (3 oz.)
1/2 cup slivered almonds
4 Tbsp. butter, melted

Preheat oven to 375 degrees.
Using a non-stick cooking spray, grease a 9 x 13-inch baking dish.

In a large saucepan, combine first 8 ingredients.
Cook over medium heat (stirring constantly) until hot.

Pour into baking dish.

Separate crescent rolls into 2 rectangles.
Place over mixture.

In a small bowl, combine remaining ingredients.
Pour over dough.

Bake (uncovered) 10-15 minutes (crust should be golden brown).

Serves 6.

TURKEY TRIANGLES

A good "after Thanksgiving" dish.

1 can (8-ct.) crescent rolls

2 cups cooked turkey, chopped
1/4 cup onion, chopped
1/4 cup celery, chopped
1/4 tsp. ground red pepper
1/4 tsp. Italian seasoning
1/4 cup mayonnaise

1 can (10¾ oz.) cream of chicken soup
1/2 soup can of milk
1 tsp. black pepper

Preheat oven to 400 degrees.

Separate crescent rolls into triangles.
Arrange 4 triangles on pan (15x10x1).

In a bowl, combine next 6 ingredients.
Mix thoroughly.
Spoon mixture onto triangles.
Lay second triangle on top. Crimp to seal edges.
Bake 10-12 minutes (until brown).

Meanwhile:
In a saucepan, combine next 3 ingredients.
Heat thoroughly (stirring frequently).

Pour over turkey triangles and serve.

VEGETABLES

BEAN PARMESANO

1/2 stick butter
2 onions, chopped

2 lbs. frozen French-style green beans, thawed
1 cup sour cream
1 can (10¾ oz.) cream of celery soup
1/2 tsp. salt
1/2 tsp. black pepper
1/2 soup can of milk

6 oz. fresh Parmesan cheese, grated

Preheat oven to 325 degrees.
Using a non-stick cooking spray, grease a 2-qt. casserole dish.

Melt butter in saucepan.
Simmer onions until transparent.

Add next 6 ingredients.

Place in casserole dish.
Sprinkle cheese on top.
Bake (uncovered) 30 minutes.

Serves 8.

CREAMED ASPARAGUS

2 cans (15 oz. size) asparagus, undrained

1 Tbsp. butter
1 Tbsp. flour

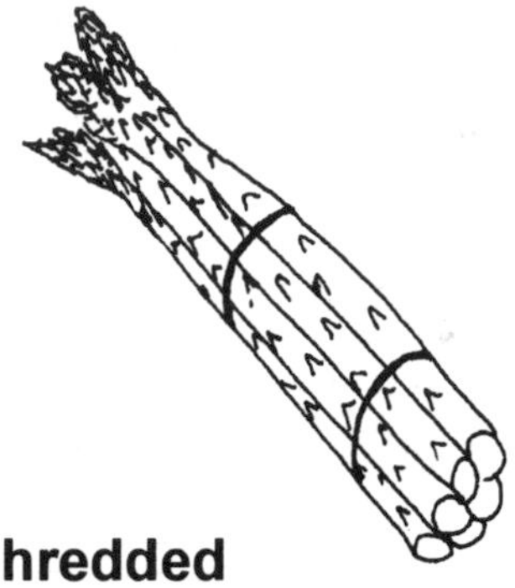

1 cup milk

1/4 tsp. salt
1/2 tsp. black pepper

1/2 cup cheddar cheese, shredded

In a saucepan, heat asparagus.

Meanwhile:
In a second saucepan, melt better over medium heat.
Stir in flour.

Gradually add milk, stirring constantly.
Cook until slightly thickened.

Stir in salt and pepper.

Add cheese.
Stir until cheese melts.

Remove asparagus to serving dish.
Top with cheese sauce.

Serves 4.

❤

LIMA BEAN BAKE

1 pkg. (16 oz.) frozen lima beans

1/2 lb. bacon

1 Tbsp. cornstarch
1/4 cup cold water

1 Tbsp. prepared mustard
3 Tbsp. brown sugar
2 Tbsp. molasses

Cook lima beans according to package directions.

Meanwhile:
Fry bacon. Crumble and set aside.

Preheat oven to 350 degrees.
Using a non-stick cooking spray, grease a 1½-qt. baking dish.

Drain beans when tender.

Dissolve cornstarch in cold water. Add to beans.
Cook until thickened.

Add bacon and remaining ingredients.
Mix thoroughly. Pour into baking dish.

Bake (uncovered) 30 minutes.

Serves 4.

STRING BEAN BAKE

2 pkgs. (10 oz. size) frozen French-style green beans

4 Tbsp. butter
1/2 cup onion, chopped
1 cup mushrooms, chopped

4 Tbsp. flour

1 cup sour cream

2 tsp. salt
1/2 tsp. black pepper
1/2 tsp. dry mustard
1 tsp. Worcestershire sauce

1 cup cheddar cheese, grated

Preheat oven to 350 degrees.
Using a non-stick cooking spray, grease a 1½-qt. baking dish.

Cook beans according to package directions. Drain and set aside.

Melt butter in large saucepan.
Add next 2 ingredients.

Cook until onions are transparent, then remove from heat.

Stir in flour.

Stir in sour cream.

Cook over low heat, stirring constantly, 3 minutes.
(Do not boil!)

Add next 4 ingredients and blend thoroughly.

Add beans to sauce and toss gently until well coated.
Turn into baking dish.
Sprinkle with grated cheese.
Bake (uncovered) 10 minutes.

Serves 8.

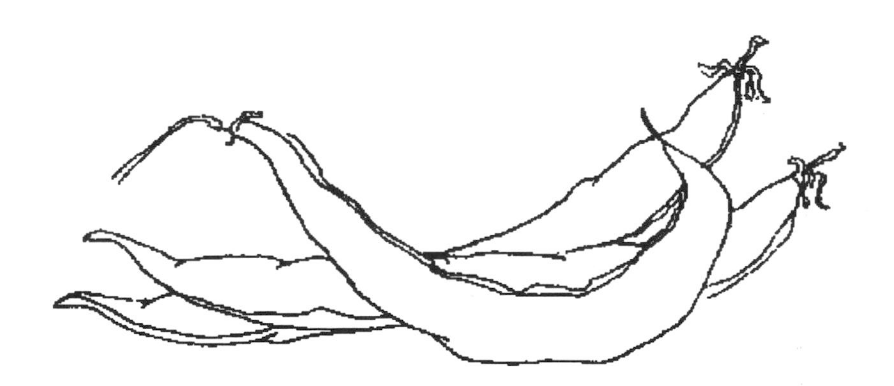

BROCCOLI CASSEROLE

Good enough to be a stand-alone meal.
This is a family favorite.

1 pkg. (16 oz.) frozen broccoli pieces

2 cans (16 oz. size) cream style corn
1/2 tsp. black pepper
2 cups Pepperidge Farm herb seasoned stuffing mix

2 cups cheddar cheese, grated

Preheat oven to 350 degrees.
Using a non-stick cooking spray, grease a 9 x 13-inch baking dish.

Cook broccoli according to package directions.
Drain and place in large bowl.

Add corn, pepper, and 1½ cups stuffing mix to broccoli.
Toss until well mixed.

Turn into baking dish.
Sprinkle remaining stuffing mix on top.

Bake (uncovered) 30 minutes.

Top with cheese.
Bake until cheese melts.

Serves 8.

BRUSSELS SPROUTS IN LEMON BUTTER

2 pkgs. (10 oz. size) frozen brussels sprouts

1/4 cup butter

1 Tbsp. lemon juice
salt
pepper

Cook brussels sprouts according to package directions.
Drain and place in serving dish.

In small saucepan, melt butter over low heat.

Add remaining ingredients.
Mix thoroughly.
Heat 2 minutes (stirring constantly).

Pour over brussels sprouts.

Serves 6.

APRICOT CARROTS

"Kids" will love eating these vegetables.

1 pkg. (16 oz.) frozen carrots

1/3 cup apricot preserves
1/2 cup orange juice
1/2 tsp. nutmeg
2 tsp. lemon juice

Cook carrots according to package directions.
Drain.

In a mixing bowl, combine remaining ingredients.
Mix thoroughly.

Pour over carrots.
Toss well.

Serves 4.

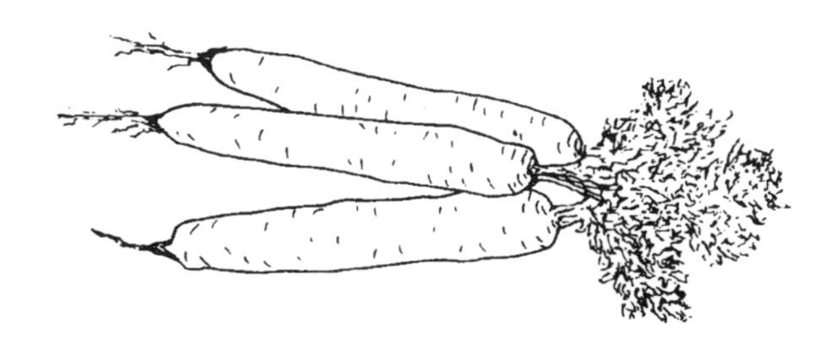

CARROTS A LA YUM

The recipe for those who hate cooked carrots.

1 lb. frozen carrots
2 Tbsp. butter
1/2 tsp. black pepper
1/4 cup sugar
1/2 tsp. nutmeg
2 cups water

Place all ingredients in a covered saucepan.
Bring to a boil.
Reduce heat and simmer 15 minutes.

Serves 6.

CAULIFLOWER AU GRATIN

3/4 cup water
2 chicken bouillon cubes

1 pkg. (16 oz.) frozen cauliflower pieces

1/2 cup Parmesan cheese*, grated

In a large covered saucepan, bring water to a boil and dissolve bouillon.

Add cauliflower.
Return to a boil.
Reduce heat and simmer (covered) 8 minutes.

Remove cauliflower to serving dish.
Sprinkle with cheese.

* *Freshly grated Parmesan cheese creates a totally different eating experience. You can purchase Parmesan cheese in a block in the dairy section of the grocery.*

Serves 4.

CHEESE POTATO STRATUS

Layers of culinary heaven.

3 large potatoes, peeled and sliced
salt
pepper

5 slices bacon, cooked and crumbled
1 large onion, sliced
1½ cups cheddar cheese, shredded

butter

Preheat oven to 350 degrees.
Using butter, grease a 9 x 13-inch baking dish.

Arrange potatoes in dish.
Sprinkle with salt and pepper.

Crumble bacon over potatoes.
Arrange onion slices over top.
Sprinkle with cheese.
Dot with butter.

Bake (covered) 30-45 minutes or until potatoes are soft.
Remove cover and brown.

Serves 6.

CORN PUDDING

Complements any meat.

3 cups frozen corn*, thawed

1 onion, finely chopped
1 green pepper, finely chopped

1 Tbsp. butter
3 cups milk
3 eggs, lightly beaten
1/4 tsp. salt
1/2 tsp. black pepper
dash of nutmeg
3 cups Monterey Jack cheese, grated

Preheat oven to 325 degrees.
Using a non-stick cooking spray, grease a 3-qt. casserole dish.

Place corn in a large mixing bowl.

Saute next two ingredients in butter.
Add to corn.

Add remaining ingredients except for 1/2 cup cheese.
Pour mixture into casserole dish.
Sprinkle with remaining cheese.
Bake (uncovered) until set (about 45-60 minutes).
Serve immediately.

Serves 10.

* *For a creamier texture, use canned cream style corn.*

RICE SPICE

An all-time favorite!

2 pkgs. (6 oz. size) Uncle Ben's long grain and wild rice mix

12 oz. cottage cheese, small curd
10 oz. Monterey Jack cheese with peppers, grated
ground red pepper
Tabasco

1/2 cup milk

Preheat oven to 350 degrees.
Using a non-stick cooking spray, grease a 3-qt. casserole dish.

Cook rice according to package directions.

In the casserole dish, layer rice and next 4 ingredients. *(Ground red pepper and Tabasco are quite hot. Use sparingly!)*

Pour milk over mixture.

Bake (uncovered) 40 minutes.

Serves 8-10.

MINTED ORANGE PEAS

A lovely accompaniment to pork.

1 pkg. (16 oz.) frozen green peas

1/8 tsp. salt
1/4 tsp. dried mint leaves
1/4 tsp. black pepper
1 Tbsp. butter
1 Tbsp. orange marmalade

Cook peas according to package directions. Drain.

Gently stir in remaining ingredients. Remove to serving dish.

Serves 4.

ORANGE GLAZED YAMS

This dish will eliminate all thoughts of dessert.

6 fresh yams
water

1/2 cup brown sugar
1/2 cup white sugar
1/2 cup orange juice
1 tsp. cornstarch

4 Tbsp. butter

Peel and slice yams.
Boil in water until almost tender.

Meanwhile:
Preheat oven to 350 degrees.
Using a non-stick cooking spray, grease a 9 x 13-inch baking dish.

In a saucepan, combine next 4 ingredients.
Cook over medium heat (stirring constantly) until sugar is dissolved.
Add butter.

Drain yams.
Arrange in baking dish.
Pour sauce over yams.

Bake (uncovered) 30 minutes.

Serves 6.

POTATO CROUSTILLANT

As good as stuffed potato skins . . .
and a whole lot easier.

6 Tbsp. butter

2-3 large baking potatoes, sliced (1/2-inch thick)

3/4 cup crushed corn flakes
1 cup sharp cheddar cheese, shredded
1 tsp. salt
1 tsp. black pepper
1 tsp. paprika

Preheat oven to 375 degrees.

Melt butter in 9 x 13-inch pan in oven.
Add single layer of potatoes.
Turn once in butter.

Mix remaining ingredients.
Sprinkle over potatoes.
Bake (uncovered) 30 minutes or until tender and tops are crisp.

Serves 4.

POTATO ONION WHIP

A new flavor in mashed potatoes.

6 medium potatoes
water

3/4 cup half & half*
2 Tbsp. butter
1 envelope Lipton onion soup
1 tsp. black pepper
1/2 tsp. salt

Peel and slice potatoes.
Place in a large saucepan.
Cover with water and cook (covered) until tender.
Drain and remove to mixing bowl.

Add remaining ingredients.
Whip until light and fluffy.

**Use more half & half if needed to prevent dryness.*

Serves 6.

RICE SICILIANO

1 cup rice, uncooked
1½ cups water
1 cup mozzarella cheese, shredded
1 can (16 oz.) stewed tomatoes
1 onion, chopped
1 green pepper, chopped
2 Tbsp. olive oil

Preheat oven to 350 degrees.
Using a non-stick cooking spray, grease a 2-qt. casserole dish.

Combine all ingredients in casserole dish.

Bake (uncovered) 1 hour.

Serves 6.

SPANISH CORN

Ole!

1 can (15 oz.) hot tamales, undrained

1 lb. frozen corn, thawed
1 cup Monterey Jack cheese with peppers, shredded
1/2 tsp. cumin
2 Tbsp. butter, melted

1/2 cup seasoned bread crumbs

1 cup milk

Preheat oven to 350 degrees.
Using a non-stick cooking spray, grease a 2-qt. casserole.

In a large bowl, pour tamales.
Remove wrappings and crush.

Add next 4 ingredients.
Mix thoroughly.

Spread 1/2 of mixture in casserole.
Top with 1/2 of bread crumbs.
Add remaining mixture.
Top with remaining crumbs.
Pour milk over top.

Bake (uncovered) 40 minutes or until brown.

Serves 6.

BUTTERNUT MASH

This is the only vegetable Jimmy would eat until he started college.

2 butternut squash
butter
salt
pepper

1/2 cup brown sugar
salt
pepper
butter

Preheat oven to 350 degrees.

Cut squash in half and clean out seeds.
Butter, salt, and pepper squash to taste.
Wrap in foil and bake until tender (about 1 hour).

When tender, scoop out squash from skin.
Add sugar, salt, pepper, and butter to taste.
Mash.
Serve hot.

Serves 6.

SWEET POTATO CRISP

The apples in this dish are a nice surprise.

1 large can (28 oz.) mashed sweet potatoes
1 cup milk
2 eggs
1 cup sugar
1/2 tsp. nutmeg
1/2 tsp. cinnamon
3/4 stick butter
1/2 tsp. vanilla
1 tsp. bourbon
2 apples, peeled and chopped

Topping:
3/4 cup corn flakes, slightly crushed
1/2 cup brown sugar
1/2 cup pecans, chopped
1/2 stick butter, softened

Preheat oven to 400 degrees.
Using a non-stick cooking spray, grease a 9 x 13-inch baking dish.

Mix first 10 ingredients and turn into dish.
Bake (uncovered) 45 minutes.
Remove from oven.

Mix next 4 ingredients and spread over potatoes.
Bake (uncovered) 10 minutes.

Serves 6.

FETTUCCINI

Easy to prepare and tastes as good as the most elegant restaurant's dish.

12 oz. egg noodles

1 stick butter

1 cup heavy cream
2 cups Parmesan cheese, shredded

6 oz. fresh mushrooms, sliced
black pepper

Cook noodles according to package directions. Drain.

Melt butter in large frying pan over medium heat. Add noodles.

Add next two ingredients.

Mix thoroughly until sauce coats noodles. Top with pepper and mushrooms.

Serves 6.

ZUCCHINI SPEZIE

Bet you've never eaten anything like this! Try it!

5 zucchini, sliced
1 onion, sliced
3 cups water

8 oz. bacon and horseradish dip
1 cup Parmesan cheese, grated
1/4 tsp. chives
1/2 tsp. minced garlic

seasoned croutons (crushed) for topping

Preheat oven to 350 degrees.
Using a non-stick cooking spray, grease a 9 x 13-inch baking dish.

Place first 3 ingredients in a saucepan.
Cook until tender.
Drain and place in baking dish.

In a bowl combine next 4 ingredients.
Pour over zucchini.

Top with croutons.

Bake (uncovered) 40 minutes.

Serves 4.

ZUCCHINI WITH STUFFING

3 medium zucchini
3 Tbsp. butter, melted

1 cup Pepperidge Farm herb seasoned stuffing mix

1 cup cheddar cheese, shredded

Preheat oven to 350 degrees.

Cut zucchini in half lengthwise.
Brush each piece with butter.
Wrap in foil.
Place on a cookie sheet.
Bake 30 minutes.

<u>Meanwhile</u>:
Prepare stuffing mix according to package directions.

When zucchini is ready, scoop out 1/2 of each piece.
Add to stuffing mix.
Fill squash shell with stuffing/squash mix.
Bake (uncovered) 15 minutes.

Sprinkle cheese on each.
Return to oven until cheese melts.

Serves 6.

❤

SPINACH SOUFFLE

This does not have a strong spinach flavor.
It makes an elegant presentation.

2 pkgs. (10 oz. size) frozen chopped spinach
1/2 tsp. salt
1/4 tsp. black pepper
1/2 tsp. minced garlic

4 eggs, beaten

2 cups sour cream

Parmesan cheese

Preheat oven to 350 degrees.
Using a non-stick cooking spray, grease a 1½-qt. casserole dish.

Cook spinach according to package directions with added seasonings.
Drain and cool.

Add eggs.

Fold in sour cream.

Turn into casserole dish.
Sprinkle Parmesan cheese on top.

Bake (uncovered) until firm.

Serves 6.

SUMMER SQUASH SOUFFLE

3 pieces of bacon

5 summer squash, sliced
1 green pepper, chopped
1 tsp. salt
1/2 tsp. black pepper
1 cup water

3/4 cup seasoned croutons
1/2 cup cheddar cheese, grated
1/2 cup Monterey Jack cheese, grated
3/4 cup French onion dip

2 eggs, separated

chives

Preheat oven to 350 degrees.
Using a non-stick cooking spray, grease a 2-qt. casserole dish.

Fry bacon until crisp. Remove bacon and retain drippings.
Crumble and set aside.

Place next 5 ingredients in pan with bacon drippings.
Cook until tender and drain thoroughly.
Place in large mixing bowl.

Add next 4 ingredients and bacon to squash and mix well.

Add egg yolks and mix well. Cool.

In a small bowl, beat egg whites until stiff and fold into squash.
Turn into casserole dish.
Bake (uncovered) 35 minutes.
Top with chives.

Serves 4.

SALADS

SPINACH SALAD

Nutritious, beautiful, and delicious.

1 bunch fresh spinach, cleaned and torn into bite-sized pieces
1 red onion, cut into rings
14 mushrooms, sliced
8 cherry tomatoes, halved

1 jar (8 oz.) sweet & sour sauce

6 pieces of bacon, cooked and crumbled

Place first 4 ingredients in large salad bowl.

Just before serving, warm sweet and sour sauce over low heat.
Spoon dressing over salad.

Top with crumbled bacon.

Serves 4.

GREEK SALAD

Catherine's version of the famous salad, from Tarpon Springs, Florida.

8 cups mixed salad greens (romaine, leaf, red leaf, etc.)

1 onion, cut into rings
1 green pepper, cut into strips
8 oz. radishes, sliced
2 tomatoes, cut into wedges
3 oz. anchovy fillets
1 cup feta cheese, small chunks
5 slices bacon, crumbled

Dressing:
1/2 tsp. salt
1/4 tsp. black pepper
1/8 tsp. lemon pepper
1/2 cup olive oil
2 Tbsp. wine vinegar

Clean salad greens.
Tear and place in a large bowl.

Arrange next 7 ingredients on top.

Combine ingredients for dressing in a jar.
Shake.
Pour into a cruet to serve.

Serves 8.

POTATO SALAD

5 medium potatoes, peeled
2 qts. water

4 eggs, hardboiled
1 qt. water

1 onion, chopped
5 celery stalks, chopped
3/4 cup sweet mixed pickle cubes

Dressing:
1/4 cup French salad dressing
1 cup mayonnaise
2 Tbsp. vinegar
1 Tbsp. Worcestershire sauce
1/2 tsp. paprika
1/4 tsp. chili powder
1/4 tsp celery seed
1/2 tsp. salt
1/4 tsp. lemon pepper
1/2 tsp. black pepper
1/4 tsp. ground mustard
1 Tbsp. prepared mustard

Boil potatoes in water until soft.
Cool and cube.

To boil eggs:

Place eggs in cold water.
Bring to a boil.
Remove from heat.
Cover and let stand 15 minutes.
Pour off hot water.
Cool in cold water.
Peel and chop.

In a large bowl, combine potatoes, eggs, onion, celery, and pickle.

Combine ingredients for dressing.
Mix thoroughly.

Pour over potato mixture and stir to coat.
Chill and serve.

Serves 6-8.

ZUCCHINI SALAD

2 cups pasta twists, cooked

2 cups zucchini, chopped
2 cups cherry tomatoes, halved
1 cup mushrooms, sliced

3/4 cup bottled ranch dressing

1 cup cheddar cheese, shredded
Parmesan cheese

Cook pasta per package directions.
Drain and cool.

Combine pasta and next 3 ingredients in large glass bowl.
Add dressing.
Stir and refrigerate.

Stir in cheddar cheese just before serving.
Top with Parmesan cheese.

Serves 6.

SLAW

This slaw will stay crisp up to 9 days.

1 large cabbage, shredded
4 celery stalks, finely chopped
2 onions, finely chopped
1 green pepper, finely chopped
1 sweet red pepper, finely chopped
1 cup sugar

Dressing:
1/2 cup salad oil
1/2 cup cider vinegar
2 tsp. salt
1 Tbsp. sugar

Combine first 6 ingredients and mix well.

In a saucepan, combine all dressing ingredients.
Bring to a boil, stirring constantly.
Pour over cabbage mixture.
Mix well.
Cover.
Chill. (Best if chilled 24 hours.)

Serves 10.

TACO SALAD

Better than "Taco Bell."

1 lb. hamburger
1/2 envelope dry onion soup mix

1 small head of lettuce

1 large tomato, sliced
10 black olives
1 small onion, cut into rings
3/4 cup cheddar cheese, shredded

1 cup crushed Doritos or tortilla chips

1/2 cup taco sauce
1/2 cup bottled French dressing

Cook hamburger and onion soup mix together.
Drain well and cool.

Clean lettuce. Tear and place in glass salad bowl.
Add hamburger.

Layer next 4 ingredients over hamburger.

Top with Doritos or tortilla chips.

Combine French dressing and taco sauce.
Pour over top.
Cover and chill thoroughly.

Serves 4.

TOMATO MOLD

1 can (10¾ oz.) tomato soup
1 soup can water

8 oz. cream cheese

2 envelopes Knox gelatin
1/2 cup cold water

1 cup mayonnaise
2 cups celery, chopped
1 tsp. minced onion
1/2 cup green pepper, chopped
3 hard-boiled eggs, chopped
1/4 tsp. black pepper
1/2 tsp. ground red pepper
2 Tbsp. lemon juice

In a saucepan, combine first 2 ingredients. Bring to a boil.

Reduce heat and add cream cheese.
Simmer, stirring constantly, until cheese is softened.
Beat with a wire whisk until mixture is thoroughly blended.

Soften gelatin in cold water.
Add to soup mixture and dissolve.
Cool.

Stir in remaining ingredients.
Pour into 1½-qt. mold.
Chill until firm.

Serves 8.

CHICK-A-PEA SALAD

Makes a beautiful presentation.

4 boneless chicken breasts

2 tomatoes, cut in wedges
32 snow peas, steamed
4 oz. mushrooms, sliced
2 apples, sliced, unpeeled

lettuce leaves

1/2 cup Velveeta, shredded
3/4 cup sour cream
1/2 tsp. black pepper
1/4 tsp. lemon pepper
1/2 Tbsp. celery seed

Simmer chicken, covered in water, until tender.
Cut into 1/2-inch strips.

Arrange chicken and next 4 ingredients on lettuce.

Place remaining ingredients in a saucepan.
Cook over low heat (stirring constantly) until cheese is melted.
Pour over salads.

Serves 4.

GREEN PEA SALAD

Nice salad on a hot day . . .
a pleasant change from potato salad.

4 cups elbow macaroni, cooked

2 cups frozen green peas, cooked
1 can (8 oz.) mushrooms, drained
2 celery stalks, chopped
1 onion, chopped
1/4 cup pickle relish
1/2 cup sweet mixed pickle

6 Tbsp. prepared mustard
1/2 cup mayonnaise

1/4 tsp. salt
1/2 tsp. black pepper

paprika

Cook macaroni per package directions.
Drain and cool.
Place in a large glass bowl.

Add next 6 ingredients.
Mix.

Add next 2 ingredients.
Mix.

Add salt and pepper. Mix thoroughly.
Chill.
Sprinkle with paprika just before serving.

Serves 10.

AMBROSIA

1 can (16 oz.) fruit cocktail, drained
1 can (10 oz.) mandarin oranges
2 apples, chopped
1 can (8 oz.) pineapple chunks, drained
1/2 cup sugar
1 cup miniature marshmallows
1 cup chopped pecans
1 cup coconut
1/2 cup sour cream

In a large bowl, combine all ingredients.
Mix thoroughly.
Chill and serve.

Serves 8.

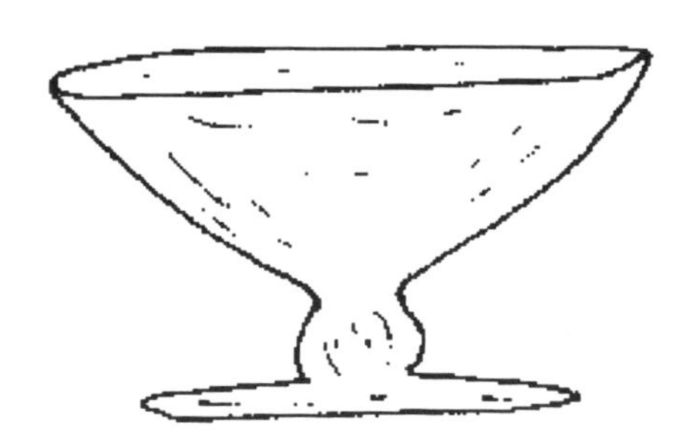

BLACK CHERRY SALAD

As good as a dessert.

1 pkg. (3 oz.) black cherry or raspberry Jello
1 cup water, boiling

1 cup 7-Up

1/2 cup crushed pineapple
1 cup black cherries*, pitted and drained
1 cup cream cheese, cubed
1/2 cup pecans, chopped

lettuce leaves
mayonnaise

Dissolve Jello in boiling water.
Add 7–Up.
Pour into a mold or dish.
Chill until partially jelled.

Add next 4 ingredients.
Chill until firm.

Serve on a bed of lettuce.
Top with mayonnaise.

**If you like more fruit, add the whole can.*

Serves 6.

FIVE-CUP SALAD

1 cup crushed pineapple, drained
1 cup coconut
1 cup mandarin oranges, drained
1 cup miniature marshmallows
1 cup sour cream

lettuce leaves

In a mixing bowl, combine first 5 ingredients. Cover and refrigerate.

Serve on lettuce leaves.

Serves 6.

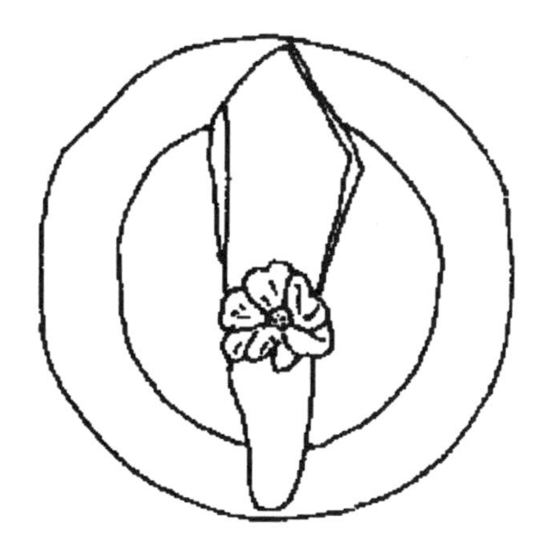

HEAVENLY HASH

2 cups Cool Whip
1 orange, peeled, seeded and diced
1 apple, cubed
1 banana, sliced
1 cup seedless grapes
1 cup crushed pineapple, drained
1 cup miniature marshmallows

1/2 cup coconut

In a large mixing bowl, combine first 7 ingredients.
Stir gently.
Cover and refrigerate.

Sprinkle with coconut when serving.

Serves 8.

LUNCHEON CHICKEN SALAD

2 cups cooked chicken, diced
1/2 cup celery, diced
1/2 cup pineapple, diced
1/2 cup mandarin oranges, drained
1/2 cup chopped walnuts

1/2 tsp. black pepper
1/2 tsp. paprika

1/2 cup mayonnaise

lettuce leaves or tomatoes

In a large mixing bowl, combine first 5 ingredients.

Sprinkle with pepper and paprika.

Add mayonnaise and toss.

Cover and refrigerate for 1 hour.

Serve on lettuce leaves or stuff tomatoes.

Serves 4.

MANDARIN ORANGE SALAD

1 pkg. (6 oz.) orange Jello
1½ cups boiling water

1 can (6 oz.) frozen orange juice
1 can (15 oz.) crushed pineapple, undrained
1 can (16 oz.) mandarin oranges, drained

1 pkg. (3.9 oz.) lemon instant pudding
1 cup milk

2 cups Cool Whip

Dissolve Jello in boiling water.

Add next three ingredients.
Congeal.

Mix next 2 ingredients slowly with mixer until well blended.

Fold the Cool Whip into the pudding mixture.
Spread over the congealed Jello.
Chill and serve.

Serves 8.

PINEAPPLE MOLD

Is it a salad or a dessert? Hard to say!

1 pkg. (3 oz.) lemon Jello
juice from crushed pineapple

3 oz. cream cheese, softened

1 can (15 oz.) crushed pineapple, juice separated
1/2 cup celery, finely chopped
2/3 cups walnuts, coarsely chopped

1/2 pt. whipping cream

Add water to pineapple juice to equal 1 cup.
Bring to a boil.
Dissolve Jello in juice.

Add cream cheese and blend.
Chill until thickened.

Add next 3 ingredients.

Whip cream.
Fold into Jello mixture.

Chill until firm.

Serves 8.

RICE AND APPLE SALAD

2 cups cooked rice
1 cup canned applesauce
1/2 cup chopped celery
3/4 cup chopped walnuts
1 cup chopped apple

6 oz. cream cheese, softened
3/4 cup sour cream
1 tsp. cinnamon
1/4 tsp. nutmeg

Combine first 5 ingredients in a large bowl.

Place next 4 ingredients in a blender.
Blend thoroughly.
Add to rice mixture and stir.
Chill and serve.

Serves 8.

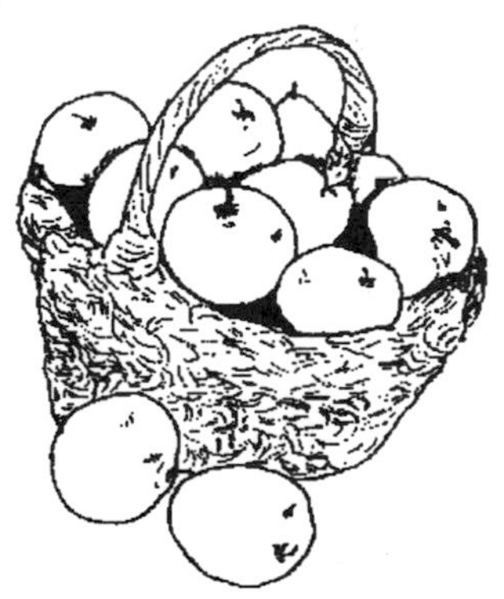

DESSERTS

GERMAN APPLE CAKE

2 eggs
2 cups all purpose flour
2 tsp. cinnamon
1 tsp. baking soda
1/2 tsp. salt
1 cup oil
1 tsp. vanilla
2 cups sugar
1 cup pecans, chopped
4 cups tart apples, chopped

2 cups Cool Whip
1/2 cup coconut

Preheat oven to 350 degrees.
Grease and flour a 9 x 13-inch baking pan.

Mix first 10 ingredients with a spoon. **Do not use mixer!**
Spread into baking pan.
Bake 45-60 minutes.

Frost with Cool Whip.
Sprinkle coconut on top.

CHOCOLATE CAKE EXTRAORDINAIRE

It really is!

1 chocolate cake mix
1 pkg. (3.9 oz.) chocolate instant pudding
1/2 cup oil
1/2 cup coffee, strong
8 oz. sour cream
4 eggs

12 oz. chocolate chips

Preheat oven to 350 degrees.
Using shortening, grease a bundt pan.

Mix first 6 ingredients with a mixer for 5 minutes.

Stir in chocolate chips.
Turn into pan.

Bake 65 minutes.

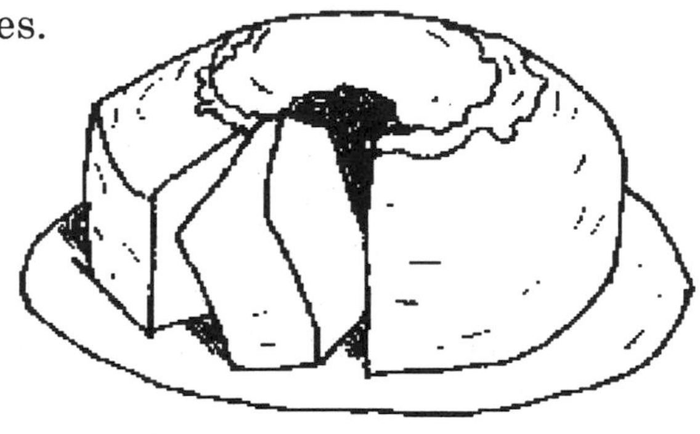

LEMONADE CAKE

Here's something a little unusual.

1 pkg. (3 oz.) lemon Jello
3/4 cup hot water

1 white cake mix
4 eggs
3/4 cup oil

1 can (6 oz.) frozen lemonade concentrate
1 cup sugar

Preheat oven to 300 degrees.
Grease and flour a bundt pan.

Dissolve Jello in hot water and set aside to cool. Do not jell.

In a large bowl, mix next 3 ingredients.
Add cooled Jello.
Beat 3 minutes.

Turn into bundt pan.
Bake 1 hour.

Meanwhile:
Mix next 2 ingredients and let set.

While cake is still warm, loosen it from edges of pan, but leave in pan. Pour lemonade mixture over cake, allowing it to run down the sides.

RUM CAKE

1/2 cup pecans, chopped

1 yellow cake mix
1 pkg. (3.9 oz.) instant vanilla pudding
1/2 cup water
4 eggs
1/2 cup light rum
1 cup oil

Glaze:
1 cup sugar
1 stick butter
1/4 cup rum
1/4 cup water

Preheat oven to 325 degrees.
Using shortening, grease and flour a bundt pan.

Sprinkle nuts in bottom of pan.

In large mixing bowl, blend next 6 ingredients.
Beat well.
Pour into bundt pan.
Bake 50-60 minutes.

In a saucepan, combine remaining ingredients.
Bring to a boil, stirring constantly.
Boil 2 minutes.
While cake is still warm, loosen it from edges of pan, but leave in pan.
Pour glaze over cake, allowing it to run down the sides.

TOFFEE CAKE

Butterfinger bars may be substituted for a less brittle crunch.

1 angel food cake

1 carton (1/2 gallon) vanilla ice cream

14 small Heath bars, crushed
1 cup walnut pieces
2 cups Cool Whip

Slice cake into two layers.

Slice ice cream and place on bottom layer of cake. Replace cake top.

Fold crushed Heath bars and walnut pieces into Cool Whip.
Ice cake with mixture.

Refrigerate.

TURTLE CAKE

If you like turtle candy, try this one.

1 German chocolate cake mix

1 bag (14 oz.) caramels
3/4 cup butter
1/2 cup evaporated milk

1 cup pecans, chopped
1 cup chocolate chips

1/2 cup chocolate chips

Preheat oven to 350 degrees.
Using shortening, grease and flour a 9 x 13 inch baking pan.

Mix cake according to directions.
Pour half into cake pan and bake 15 minutes.

Meanwhile:
In a saucepan, combine next 3 ingredients.
Heat over low heat (stirring constantly) until caramels are melted.
Set aside.

Remove cake from oven.

Top with next 2 ingredients and caramel mixture.

Pour second half of cake batter over top.

Bake 20 minutes.

In a saucepan, melt 1/2 cup of chocolate chips over low heat.
Drizzle over cake top.

BANANA NUT BREAD

1/2 cup shortening

1 cup sugar

2 eggs

3 bananas, crushed

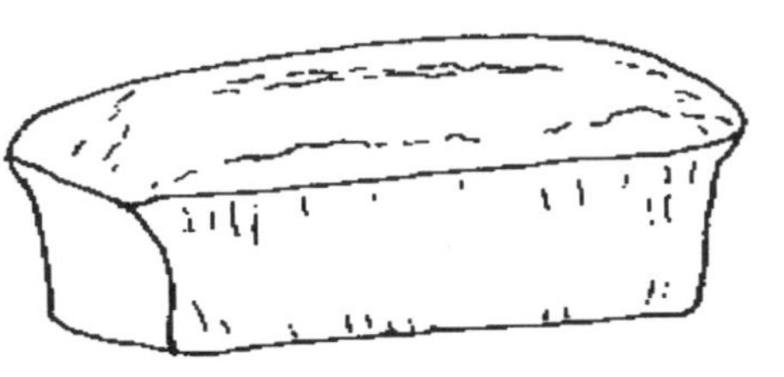

2 cups all purpose flour

1 tsp. baking soda
1/4 tsp. salt

1/2 cup walnuts, chopped

Preheat oven to 350 degrees.
Using shortening, grease and flour a loaf pan or muffin tins.

With a mixer, cream shortening.
Add sugar and beat until smooth.

Add eggs one at a time. Mix thoroughly.

Gradually add bananas while beating.

Reduce speed and add flour a cup at a time.

Add next 2 ingredients.

Fold in nuts.

Turn into loaf pan or muffin tins.

Bake 40 minutes for loaf pan.
Bake 25 minutes for 2-inch muffin tins.
Bake 20 minutes for mini-muffins.

APPLE CRUMB PIE

You can't get more "American" than this.

1 frozen deep-dish pie shell, thawed

3 cups tart apple slices

1 tsp. cinnamon
1/8 tsp. salt

1/2 cup all purpose flour
1/2 cup cookie crumbs
1/2 tsp. cinnamon
1/4 cup brown sugar
1 Tbsp. butter, melted

Preheat oven to 350 degrees.

Arrange apples in pie shell.
Sprinkle with next 2 ingredients.

In a mixing bowl, combine next 5 ingredients.
Mix well.
Sprinkle over apples.

Bake 1 hour.

BLUEBERRY CHEESECAKE PIE

Sinful!

1 frozen pie shell

1 pkg. (8 oz.) cream cheese, softened
1 cup confectioner's sugar
1 tsp. vanilla

1 cup Cool Whip

1 can (15 oz.) blueberry pie filling

Bake pie shell according to package directions. Cool.

In a large mixing bowl, combine next 3 ingredients. Beat until smooth.

Fold in Cool Whip.
Pour into pie shell.

Spoon pie filling carefully over cheese layer.

Chill until set.

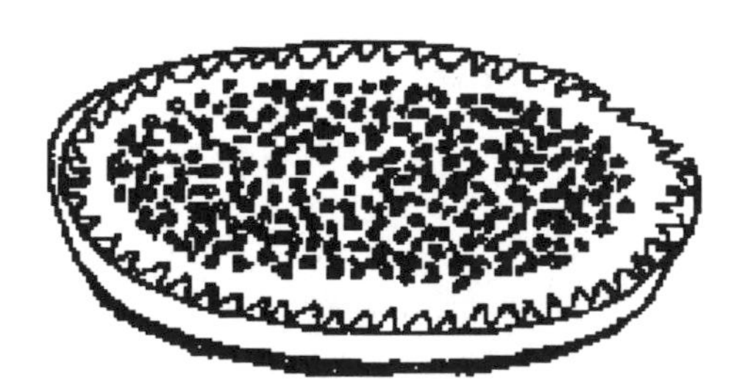

ICE BOX PIE

2 pkgs. (8 oz.) cream cheese, softened
1 cup chopped pecans

1 graham cracker crust

1 can (16 oz.) cherry pie filling

2 cups Cool Whip

Stir nuts into softened cream cheese.
Spread over pie shell.

Pour cherry pie filling over cream cheese.

Spread with Cool Whip.

Chill and serve.

COCONUT PIE

This pie makes its own crust.

4 eggs
1¼ cups sugar
1/2 cup self-rising flour

2 cups milk
1 tsp. vanilla
1 can (7 oz.) flake coconut

Preheat oven to 350 degrees.
Using a non-stick cooking spray, grease 9-inch (deep dish) glass pie pan.

Beat eggs.
Blend in sugar and flour.

Add remaining ingredients.

Pour into pie pan.
Bake 30-40 minutes.

OLD-FASHIONED COOKIE PIE

3 egg whites

1/4 tsp. salt
1 tsp. baking powder
3/4 cup sugar

7 chocolate cream-filled cookies, crushed
1/2 cup pecans, chopped
1/2 cup coconut, shredded

Cool Whip

Preheat oven to 325 degrees.
Grease an 8 x 8-inch baking pan.

Beat egg whites until fluffy.

Add next 3 ingredients.
Beat until stiff.

Fold in next 2 ingredients and 1/2 of coconut.
Pour into pan.
Sprinkle top with remaining coconut.
Bake 30 minutes.

Serve with Cool Whip.

PECAN PIE

Like Mom used to make.

3 eggs
1/2 cup butter, melted
3/4 cup sugar
1 cup dark Karo syrup
1 tsp. vanilla
1 tsp. vinegar

1 cup pecans, chopped

1 uncooked pie shell

pecan halves, for top of pie

Preheat oven to 300 degrees.

Mix first 6 ingredients.

Add pecans.
Pour into pie shell.

Arrange pecan halves on top of pie.

Bake 45-60 minutes.
(Pie is done when knife stuck in center comes out clean.)

PUMPKIN PIE

This pie makes its own crust.

3/4 cup sugar
1/2 cup Bisquick
2 Tbsp. butter
1 can (12 oz.) evaporated milk
1 can (16 oz.) pumpkin
2½ tsp. pumpkin pie spice
2 tsp. vanilla

Preheat oven to 350 degrees.
Using a non-stick cooking spray, grease a deep-dish pie plate.

In a large mixing bowl*, combine all ingredients.
Mix well.
Turn into pie plate.

Bake 45-50 minutes.

**May be done in blender.*

RAISIN PIE

The "8th Wonder of the World!"

1 cup sugar
1/2 cup raisins
1/2 cup pecans, chopped
1 Tbsp. lemon juice
1/4 tsp. ground cloves
1/2 tsp. cinnamon
1 Tbsp. butter, melted
1 Tbsp. water

2 eggs, beaten

1 frozen pie shell, uncooked

Preheat oven to 450 degrees.
Remove pie shell from freezer to thaw.

In a large mixing bowl, combine first 8 ingredients by hand.
Stir well.

Add beaten eggs.
Stir. *(Don't worry! Mixture will thicken as it cooks.)*

Pour into unbaked pie shell.

Bake 5 minutes at 450 degrees.
Reduce heat to 350 degrees and bake 30 minutes.

STRAPPLE PIE

1 frozen pie shell, thawed

2 apples, peeled and sliced
2 cups strawberries, sliced

3 egg yolks

1/2 cup sugar

1/2 cup flour
1/2 tsp. cinnamon
1/4 tsp. nutmeg
1 tsp. lemon juice

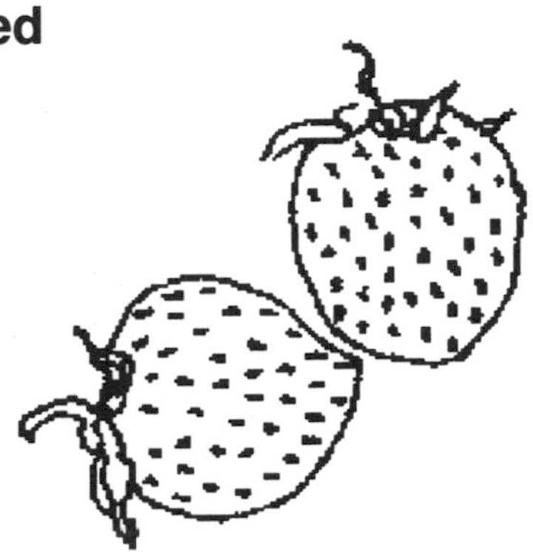

3 egg whites, beaten stiff

Cool Whip for garnish

Preheat oven to 375 degrees.

Arrange apples in pie shell.
Arrange strawberries over apples.

Beat egg yolks.
Add sugar. Whip until fluffy.

Add next 4 ingredients.
Beat until smooth.

Fold in egg whites. Pour over pie.

Bake at 375 degrees for 8 minutes.
Reduce heat to 325 degrees and bake until set.

Serve with Cool Whip.

CHOCOLATE CHEESE DESSERT

Rich and sinful!

1 stick butter or margarine
2 Tbsp. sugar
1 cup flour
1 cup pecans, chopped

12 oz. cream cheese
1 cup Cool Whip
1 cup 4X sugar

2 pkgs. (3.9 oz.) inst. chocolate pudding mix
2-2/3 cup milk

Garnish
1 cup Cool Whip
1/2 cup pecans, chopped

Preheat oven to 350 degrees.

Mix first 4 ingredients.
Pat into a 9 x 9-inch baking dish to make crust.
Bake 20 minutes.
Cool.

Mix next 3 ingredients.
Spread over crust.

Combine next 2 ingredients.

Spread over cream cheese mixture.
Chill.

Garnish with Cool Whip and chopped nuts.

APPLE STRUDEL

4 large apples*

1/4 cup sugar
2 tsp. cinnamon

4 Tbsp. butter

1 cup sugar
1 tsp. baking powder
1 cup flour
1/2 tsp. salt

1 egg, beaten

Preheat oven to 350 degrees.
Using butter, grease a 9 x 13-inch baking dish.

Peel and slice apples.
Arrange in baking dish.

Combine sugar and cinnamon. Sprinkle over apples.
Dot with butter (thinly sliced).

In a mixing bowl, combine next 4 ingredients.
Mix well.

Add egg.
Mix until crumbly.
Sprinkle over apples.

Bake until crust is brown.

**Peaches may be substituted.*

BAKED APRICOTS

2 sticks butter or margarine, melted
1 can (28 oz.) apricot halves, drained
2 cups light brown sugar
1 box (11.46 oz.) Ritz crackers, crushed

Preheat oven to 300 degrees.

Layer ingredients in a 2-qt. casserole dish:

1/3 of the butter
1/2 of the apricots
1 cup of sugar
1/2 of the crackers

1/3 of the butter
1/2 of the apricots
1 cup of sugar
1/2 of the crackers

1/3 of the butter

Bake (uncovered) for 1 hour.

PEACH A LA ORANGE

Makes a nice garnish for beef and pork dishes.

1 large can (28 oz.) peach halves, drained
3 tsp. brown sugar
3 tsp. pecans, chopped
cinnamon
1/4 cup orange juice
butter

Preheat the broiler.
Butter a 9 x 9-inch baking pan.

Place peach halves in pan.

Put 1/2 tsp. brown sugar in each.

Put 1/2 tsp. pecans in each.

Sprinkle with cinnamon.

Drizzle orange juice over each.

Put a thick pat of butter on top of each.

Broil 10 to 15 minutes.
Watch carefully so as not to burn.

PEACH COBBLER

Blackberries work just as well in this recipe.

1 stick butter

3/4 cup sugar
3/4 cup milk
3/4 cup self-rising flour

1 can (28 oz.) sliced peaches, drained

Preheat oven to 350 degrees.
Melt butter in a 9 x 9-inch baking pan.

In a bowl, combine next 3 ingredients.
Pour over melted butter.

Spoon peaches on top.

Bake 1 hour.

RASPBERRY CRUNCH

A nice change from pie and cake.

1 pkg. (7 oz.) vanilla wafers, crushed

1 carton (8 oz.) whipped cream cheese
1½ cups powdered sugar
1 cup sour cream

2 cups Cool Whip
1 cup pecans, chopped
1 pkg. frozen raspberries, thawed and well drained

Place 1/2 of the crushed vanilla wafers in a 9 x 9-inch pan.

Blend next 3 ingredients.
Spread on top of wafers.

Mix next 3 ingredients.
Spread on top of cheese mixture.

Top with remaining vanilla wafers.
Refrigerate.

APPETIZERS

BACON CHESTNUTS

A deliciously crisp experience.

1 can (8 oz.) whole water chestnuts, drained
1/4 cup soy sauce
1 Tbsp. sugar

1/2 lb. bacon

In a small bowl, combine first 3 ingredients.
Marinate 30 minutes.

Preheat oven to 375 degrees.
Using a non-stick cooking spray, grease a roasting rack and baking pan.

Cut bacon slices into thirds.
Wrap bacon around water chestnuts.
Secure with toothpicks.
Arrange on roasting rack in baking pan.

Bake 20-25 minutes (until bacon is crisp).

Makes 20.

BACON ROLL-UPS

Excellent and easy to make.

1 can Pillsbury crescent dinner rolls
1 cup sour cream
1 lb. bacon, cooked and crumbled

Preheat oven to 375 degrees.

Unroll and cut each triangle into 3 small triangles.
Brush each triangle with sour cream.
Sprinkle crushed bacon over each section.
Roll each triangle.

Bake 15 minutes.

CHINESE MEATBALLS

Sweet and tasty.

1 lb. hamburger
1 onion, grated
1 egg
1/2 tsp. minced garlic
1 Tbsp. Worcestershire sauce
1/2 cup Pepperidge Farm herb seasoned stuffing mix, crushed

1 bottle (8 oz.) sweet & sour sauce

Mix first 6 ingredients.
Form into 1-inch balls.
Broil, shaking occasionally to brown all sides.

Serve on toothpicks.

Dip in sweet & sour sauce.

CLAM DIP

8 oz. cream cheese, softened
1 can (3 oz.) minced clams
1/4 tsp. lemon juice
1/4 tsp. granulated garlic
1/2 tsp. minced onion
1/4 tsp. ground red pepper

Combine all ingredients.
Chill.

Serve with bread sticks.

Makes 1 cup.

This is a clam in the shell. The Lazy Cook prefers to buy clams in a can.

CRAB DIP

8 oz. cream cheese
1 can (8 oz.) crabmeat
1/2 tsp. ground red pepper
3 Tbsp. picante sauce

Combine all ingredients in a saucepan.

Cook over low heat until blended.

Serve hot with crackers.

Makes 1½ cups.

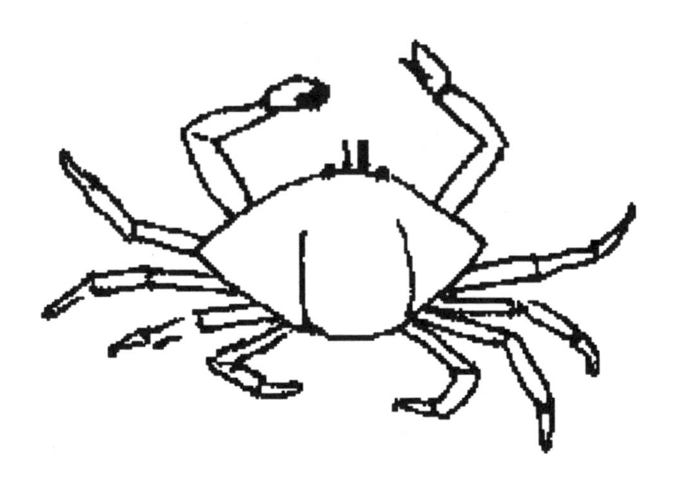

SHRIMP COCKTAIL DIP

1 frozen shrimp cocktail (4 oz.)
12 oz. cream cheese, softened

Thaw shrimp cocktail.

Stir in cream cheese.

Serve with crackers.

Makes 2 cups.

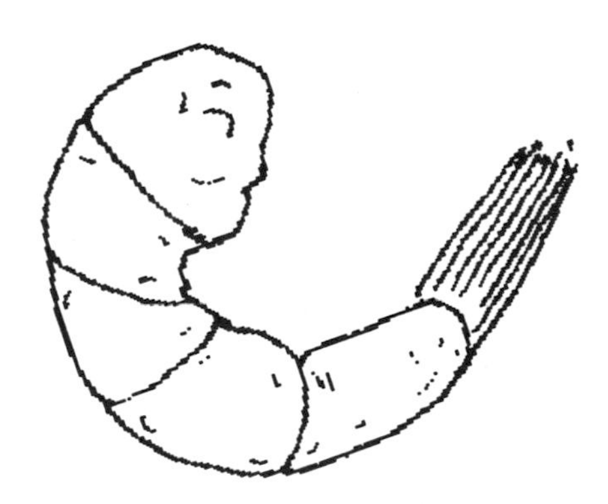

SPICY DIP

6 oz. cream cheese, softened
1/2 cup sour cream
1/4 cup chili sauce
1/2 tsp. mustard
2 Tbsp. minced onion

Blend and chill.

Serve with raw vegetables or taco chips.

Makes 1 cup.

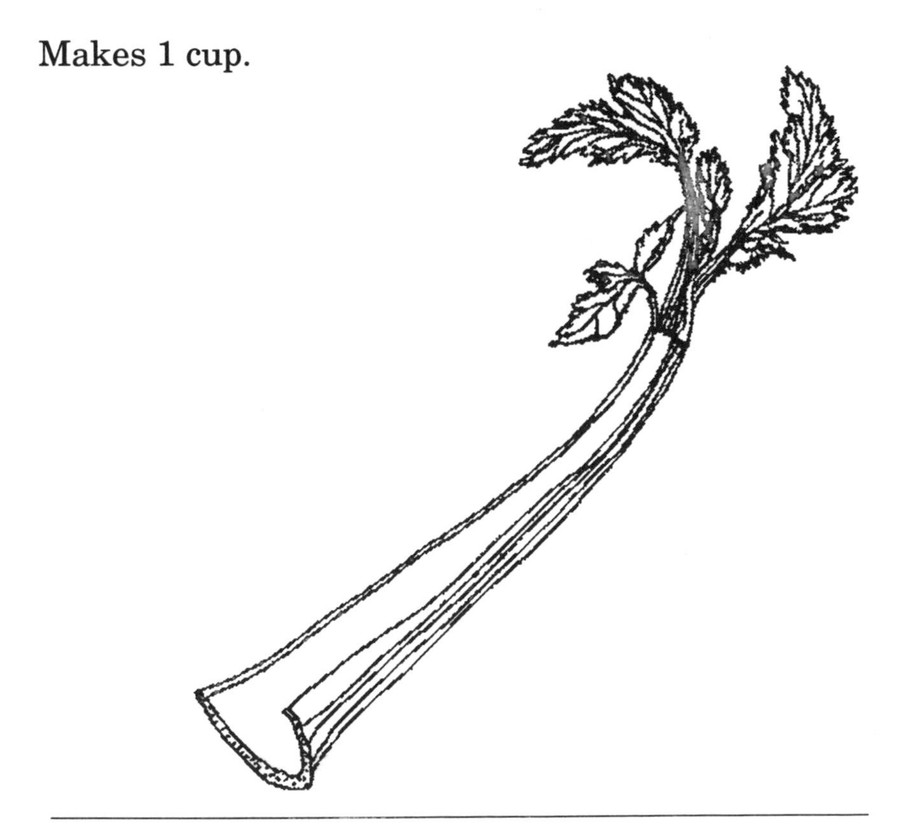

TACO DIP

This is colorful and delicious.

1 lb. ground beef

8 oz. cream cheese
1 pkg. taco seasoning mix
8 oz. taco sauce

8 oz. sour cream
1 cup of lettuce, shredded
2 tomatoes, cubed
1/2 cup black olives
1/2 lb. cheddar cheese

1 pkg. tortilla chips

Brown ground beef and drain.

Mix cream cheese, taco seasoning (to taste), and taco sauce.

Layer:
cream cheese mixture
sour cream
ground beef
lettuce
tomatoes
black olives
cheddar cheese

Serve with tortilla chips.

❤

HAM BISCUITS

1 can of biscuits

<u>Filling:</u>

1 can (2¼ oz.) deviled ham
3/4 Tbsp. mustard
1 tsp. mayonnaise

<u>Filling:</u> (optional)

1/2 cup cheddar cheese, grated
1 Tbsp. chili sauce
1 tsp. mayonnaise

Preheat oven to 400 degrees.

Blend ingredients for filling with a wire whisk.

Slice biscuits.

Spread bottom half with filling.

Replace top and bake until golden brown.

SAUCY DOGS

24 oz. pepper jelly

6 oz. Dijon mustard

2 lbs. hot dogs,
cut into bite-sized pieces

In a saucepan, melt jelly over low heat.

Add mustard.
Heat thoroughly.

Add hot dogs.
Simmer for 15 minutes.
Use toothpicks for serving.

SAUSAGE GLOBALIS

1 lb. Italian sausage

1 cup sweet & sour sauce
1 cup hot taco sauce

Slice sausage diagonally into 1-inch pieces.
Cook thoroughly in skillet.

In a saucepan, combine the remaining ingredients.
Heat thoroughly.

Place sausage in a chafing dish.
Pour sauce over.
Serve hot.

SAUSAGE BALLS

1 lb. bulk sausage
1 egg, beaten
1/3 cup seasoned bread crumbs
1/2 tsp. chili powder
1/4 tsp. ground red pepper

1/4 cup catsup
1 jar (16 oz.) Prego spaghetti sauce
1 Tbsp. soy sauce
1 Tbsp. Worcestershire sauce

Mix first 5 ingredients.
Form into 3/4-inch balls.
Broil, shaking pan occasionally, until brown on all sides.

In saucepan, combine remaining ingredients.
Add sausage balls.
Simmer (covered) 12 minutes.

CHEESE SPREAD

8 oz. cream cheese, softened
8 oz. cheddar cheese, shredded
1 pkg. Good Seasons Italian dressing mix
1/2 cup mayonnaise

Mix all ingredients thoroughly.

Serve with crackers or bread sticks.

Makes 2½ cups.

NUTS A LA PIZZAZZ

4 Tbsp. butter
1/2 tsp. seasoned salt
dash Tabasco
1/2 tsp. garlic powder

1 lb. mixed nuts

3 Tbsp. Worcestershire sauce

Preheat oven to 300 degrees.

In a small saucepan, combine first 4 ingredients.
Heat over low heat until butter melts.

Add nuts.
Toss to coat.

Turn into 9 x 13-inch baking dish.
Bake 15 minutes (stirring occasionally).

Sprinkle with Worcestershire sauce.
Bake 15 minutes (until crisp).

Makes 3-4 cups.

SOUPS

CHEESE SOUP

1 cup carrot, shredded
1/2 cup onion, chopped
1/2 cup celery, chopped
2 Tbsp. butter

1 can (10¾ oz.) cream of chicken soup
1 can (16 oz.) chicken broth
1/2 cup of milk
1/2 tsp. black pepper
dash of Tabasco
1/2 tsp. crushed red pepper

2 cups Velveeta, shredded

In a large saucepan, saute first 3 ingredients in butter.

Add next 6 ingredients.
Simmer (stirring frequently) 10 minutes.

Add cheese.
Simmer, stirring constantly, until cheese melts.

Serves 4.

❤

GARBANZO BEAN SOUP

Serve with crusty bread.

1 lb. Italian sausage, sliced into bite-sized pieces
1 onion, chopped
1 green pepper, chopped

4 cups water
1 can (15 oz.) garbanzo beans
1 cup frozen corn, thawed
2 cubes beef bouillon
1/4 tsp. lemon pepper
1/2 tsp. minced garlic
1/4 tsp. ground red pepper

Brown first 3 ingredients in large Dutch oven.

Add remaining ingredients.
Bring to a boil.
Reduce heat and simmer (covered) 30 minutes.

Serves 6.

EGG DROP SOUP

2 Tbsp. cornstarch
1/4 cup water

6 cups chicken broth
1/4 tsp. lemon pepper
1/2 tsp. granulated garlic
1 Tbsp. soy sauce

3 eggs, slightly beaten

green onions, finely chopped

chow mein noodles

Dissolve cornstarch in water. Set aside.

Combine next 4 ingredients in saucepan.
Bring to a boil.

Slowly pour eggs into pan (stirring constantly).
Boil 3 minutes.

Add green onions.
Cook 2 minutes.

Add cornstarch mixture slowly (stirring constantly).
Cook (stirring constantly) until soup thickens.

Garnish individual servings with chow mein noodles.

Serves 6.

RIVVEL SOUP

An excellent choice to serve as a prelude to a heavy meal. Flavor resembles chicken and dumplings.

2 qts. chicken broth

1¼ cups flour
1/2 tsp. salt
1 egg, well beaten

1 cup corn

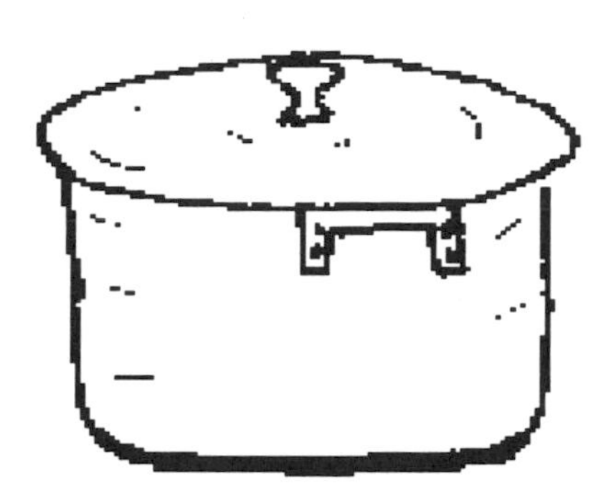

In a large stock pot, bring chicken broth to boil.

Meanwhile:
In a bowl, combine flour, salt and egg.
Mix with fingers until crumbly.

Drop rivvels (crumbs) into boiling broth.

Add corn.

Simmer 10-15 minutes. Stir occasionally to prevent rivvels from forming a mass.

Does not reheat well!

Serves 6.

CHICKEN CORN SOUP

Our friends, Jeannette and Jerry, love this soup.

4 lbs. chicken (whole or pieces)
4 qts. water
1 onion, chopped
1/4 tsp. salt
1/4 tsp. black pepper
1/2 tsp. lemon pepper

2 cups corn
1/2 cup celery, chopped

2 hard-boiled eggs, sliced (minus yolks)

Rivvels:
1 cup flour
1 egg
salt
milk (optional)

Bring first 6 ingredients to a boil and reduce heat.
When chicken is tender, remove bones.
Return meat to broth.
Add corn and celery.
Simmer 20 minutes.
Return to boil.

Meanwhile:
Combine ingredients for rivvels.
Mix to form small crumbs. (If more liquid is needed, add milk.)
Drop rivvels slowly (stirring) into soup.
Add eggs.

Reduce heat and simmer an additional 15 minutes. Stir frequently to prevent rivvels from forming a mass.

Serves 8.

CORN CHOWDER

Very satisfying on a cool day.

2 cups potatoes, diced
3/4 cup carrots, thinly sliced
1/2 cup celery, finely chopped
1/4 tsp. black pepper
1/8 tsp. salt
4 cups water

2 cans (10¾ oz. size) cream of chicken soup
2 cups milk

2 cups cheddar cheese, shredded

1 can (16 oz.) cream style corn

Combine first 6 ingredients in heavy Dutch oven.
Bring to a boil.
Reduce heat.
Simmer (covered) until vegetables are tender.

Meanwhile:
In a saucepan, combine next 2 ingredients and heat thoroughly.
Melt cheese in soup.
Add corn.

When vegetables are tender, add mixture to vegetables. (Do not drain vegetables.)
Stir and serve.

Serves 6.

BROCCOLI SOUP

1 lb. frozen chopped broccoli
1 cup frozen carrots
1 onion, chopped
1/4 tsp. lemon pepper
2 cups water

2 cans (10¾ oz. size) cream of celery soup
1 can (16 oz.) chicken broth
1/2 tsp. black pepper
1/4 tsp. minced garlic

Combine first 5 ingredients in large saucepan.
Bring to a boil.
Reduce heat and simmer (covered) 8 minutes.

Stir in remaining ingredients.
Simmer 10 minutes (stirring frequently).

Serves 8.

COLLARD GREEN SOUP

This is a Spanish soup.

1/2 lb. kielbasa, sliced
3 potatoes, diced
1 onion, chopped
1 green pepper, chopped
1/8 tsp. black pepper
1/8 tsp. ground mustard
6 cups water

1 can (16 oz.) navy beans
1½ cups frozen collard greens

Bring first 7 ingredients to a boil.
Reduce temperature and simmer (covered) 25 minutes.

Add remaining ingredients.

Simmer (covered) 25 minutes.

Serves 6.

SQUASH SOUP

2 yellow squash, sliced
2 zucchini, sliced
1 cup celery, chopped
1 cup carrots, sliced
3 Tbsp. butter

4 cups chicken broth
1/2 tsp. black pepper
1/4 tsp. sweet basil
1/4 tsp. lemon pepper

bacon bits for garnish (optional)

Saute first 4 ingredients in butter until soft.
Liquefy in blender.

Combine with next 4 ingredients.
Heat to boiling point.
Serve hot or cold.

Garnish with bacon bits (optional).

Serves 4.

COLD CUCUMBER SOUP

Refreshing in warm weather.

1 can (10¾ oz.) tomato soup
1 can (10¾ oz.) chicken gumbo soup
1 soup can of water
1 Tbsp. of vinegar
1 garlic bud
2 cucumbers (sliced very thin)

Combine ingredients.
Chill overnight.
Remove garlic bud before serving.

Serves 6.

GAZPACHO

1 cup tomato juice
1 cup crushed ice
1/8 tsp. black pepper
1/2 tsp. minced garlic
1/4 cup chopped onion
2 Tbsp. wine vinegar
2 Tbsp. olive oil
dash of Tabasco sauce

1/4 green pepper
1 cucumber, peeled and sliced
2 tomatoes, peeled and quartered

Blend (in blender) first 8 ingredients until the ice disappears.

Add remaining ingredients.
Blend until coarsely chopped.

Chill and serve.

Serves 4.

FRENCH ONION SOUP

4 large onions, thinly sliced
1/2 stick butter

1/2 tsp. paprika
1 Tbsp. flour
2 tsp. Worcestershire sauce

6 cups beef bouillon

seasoned croutons
Parmesan cheese*, grated

In a heavy stock pot, saute onions in butter.

Sprinkle next 3 ingredients over onions.
Cook 3 minutes (stirring frequently).

Slowly add bouillon (stirring constantly) until soup begins to boil.
Reduce heat.
Cover and simmer 20 minutes.

Top with croutons and Parmesan cheese when serving.

* *Use fresh Parmesan. It will be located in the dairy section of your market.*

Serves 4.

CREAM OF POTATO SOUP

This recipe is more trouble than others, but well worth the effort.

6 potatoes, chopped
2 onions, chopped
1 carrot, thinly sliced
2 celery stalks, thinly sliced

2 cups water
1/4 tsp. salt
1/2 tsp. celery seed
1/8 tsp. basil

Cream Sauce:
4 Tbsp. butter
1/4 cup flour
2 cups milk

Optional:
freshly ground black pepper
shredded cheddar cheese

Peel potatoes, onions, and carrot. Clean celery. Chop vegetables (1/2 inch).

Bring to a boil (covered) in water with seasonings. Reduce heat, simmer until tender (about 30 minutes).

Meanwhile, make cream sauce:
Melt butter over low heat.
Add flour. Stir constantly until smooth.
Add milk slowly.
Cook, stirring constantly, until sauce thickens.

Add cream sauce to vegetables and water.

Top with freshly ground black pepper and shredded cheese (optional).

Serves 6.

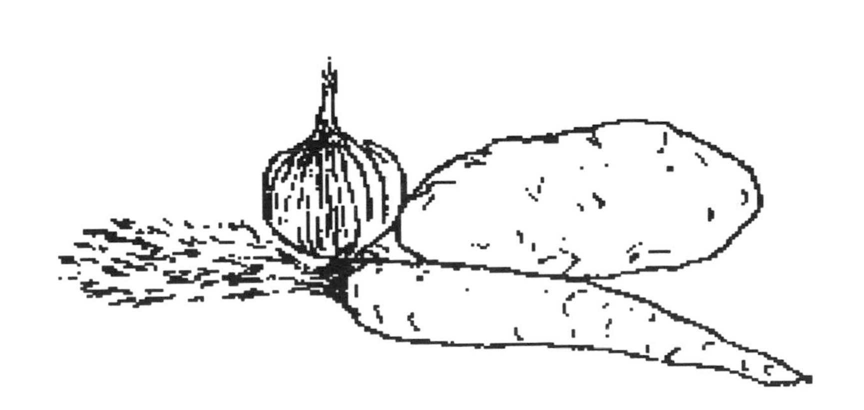

HAM-VEGETABLE CHOWDER

3 cups water

4 potatoes, peeled and cubed
1 cup celery, chopped
1 cup carrots, chopped
1 onion, chopped
2 tsp. salt
1 tsp. black pepper

2 cans (10¾ oz. size) cream of chicken soup
2 cups milk

4 cups shredded sharp cheddar cheese

2 cups cubed cooked ham

In a heavy Dutch oven, bring water to a boil.
Add next 6 ingredients.
Reduce heat. Cover and simmer until vegetables are soft.

Stir in next 2 ingredients.
Heat thoroughly.

Add cheese.
Stir constantly until cheese melts.

Stir in ham.

Serves 8.

COUNTRY VEGETABLE GOULASH

A meal in itself.

1 lb. ground beef
dash of Worcestershire sauce

1 medium onion, chopped
2 cups potatoes, cubed
8 cups water
1 can (16 oz.) whole tomatoes
1/4 cup catsup
2 beef bouillon cubes
1 cup frozen carrots
1 cup frozen green peas
1 cup frozen green beans
1 cup frozen okra
1 cup frozen whole kernel corn
1 tsp. salt
1 tsp. black pepper
1 tsp. sugar
1 bay leaf

In a large stock pot, brown hamburger with Worcestershire sauce. Drain excess fat.

Add remaining ingredients.
Bring to a boil.
Reduce heat and simmer 45 minutes.

Remove bay leaf before serving.

Serves 4 - 6.

❤

SPLIT PEA SOUP

1/2 lb. dried split peas
7 cups water

1/2 cup carrots, diced
1/2 cup celery, chopped
1/2 cup onion, chopped
1/2 cup ham, chopped
3 Tbsp. butter

1/4 tsp. salt
1/2 tsp. black pepper
1/2 tsp. granulated garlic

Wash split peas.
Bring to a boil

Saute next 4 ingredients in butter.
Add to peas.

Add remaining ingredients and reduce heat.
Cook (stirring occasionally) until peas come apart (about 1½ hours).

Serves 6.

SAUSAGE SOUP

Tasty and Satisfying!

1 lb. pork sausage

1 can (16 oz.) kidney beans, undrained
1 can (16 oz.) stewed tomatoes
6 cups water
1 onion, chopped
2 cups potatoes, sliced very thin
2 cups cabbage, shredded
1/4 tsp. minced garlic
1/2 tsp. lemon pepper
1/4 tsp. ground red pepper
dash of Tabasco
1/2 tsp. celery seed
2 beef bouillon cubes

Brown sausage and drain.

Combine all ingredients in large stock pot. Simmer until vegetables are tender.

Serves 8.

KIELBASA SOUP

A hearty soup, excellent served with warm bread.

1 lb. Kielbasa (Polish sausage), sliced
1 cup celery (1½ large stalks), chopped
1 onion, chopped

8 cups water
3 beef bouillon cubes

16 oz. frozen green beans
8 oz. frozen whole kernel corn
8 oz. frozen okra
1/4 tsp. chili powder
1 tsp. Italian seasoning

2 Tbsp. cornstarch
1/4 cup cold water

1 cup Monterey Jack cheese with peppers, shredded

In a non-stick pan, saute first 3 ingredients (medium heat) until onion is clear.

Meanwhile:

In a large stock pot, bring water to a boil and dissolve bouillon in water.

Add next 5 ingredients and cook (covered) 5 minutes.

❤

Add kielbasa, celery, and onion.
Reduce heat and simmer (covered) 20 minutes.

Dissolve cornstarch in water.

Add slowly to soup, stirring constantly.
Cook till soup thickens (2-3 minutes).

Sprinkle cheese on individual servings.

Serves 6.

CRAB BISQUE

1 lb. crabmeat
1 can (10¾ oz.) tomato soup
1 can (10¾ oz.) green pea soup
1 cup chicken broth
1/4 tsp. black pepper
1/4 tsp. ground red pepper

1/2 cup sherry

Combine first 6 ingredients in a large saucepan. Bring to a boil.

Reduce heat and simmer (covered) 10 minutes.

Add sherry and serve.

Serves 4.

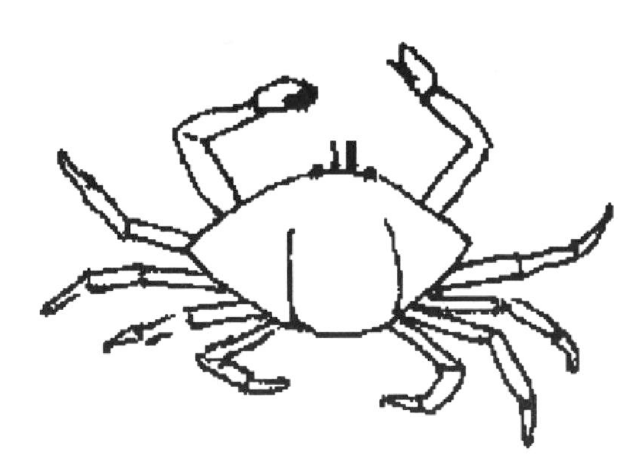

OYSTER STEW

1 can (10¾ oz.) cream of celery soup
1 cup milk
1/4 tsp. basil
1/2 tsp. minced garlic

8 oz. canned oysters

1/3 cup sherry

Combine first 4 ingredients in saucepan.
Bring to a boil very slowly.
Reduce heat.

Add oysters.
Simmer 5 minutes.

Add sherry and serve.

Serves 4.

CLAM CHOWDER

1/4 cup onion, diced
1/4 cup bacon, chopped

14 oz. canned clams

2 cups potatoes, diced
1/2 cup water
clam liquid (drained from clams)
1 tsp. salt
1/8 tsp. black pepper
1/4 tsp. celery seed
dash of ground red pepper

2 cups milk

In a large Dutch oven, cook first two ingredients.

Drain clams and set aside. Save liquid.

Add next 7 ingredients.
Simmer (covered) until potatoes are soft.

Add milk and clams.
Simmer (covered) 15 minutes.

Serves 6.

SUBSTITUTIONS

For best results, use what the recipe calls for. In an emergency, here is a list of substitutions that will accommodate most situations.

INGREDIENT	SUBSTITUTION
1 cup cake flour	1 cup minus 2 Tbsp. all purpose flour
1 cup self-rising flour	1 cup all purpose flour plus 1 tsp. baking powder and ½ tsp. salt
1 cup all purpose flour	1 cup plus 2 Tbsp. cake flour
1/2 cup butter	½ cup shortening plus ¼ tsp. salt
1 cup sour cream	1 Tbsp. lemon juice plus evaporated milk to equal 1 cup
1 cup tomato juice	½ cup tomato sauce plus ½ cup water
1 cup catsup *(cooking only)*	1 cup tomato sauce plus ½ cup sugar and 2 Tbsp. vinegar
1 cup yogurt	1 cup buttermilk
1 cup buttermilk	1 Tbsp. vinegar or lemon juice plus whole milk to equal 1 cup
1 cup milk	½ cup evaporated milk plus ½ cup water
1 tsp. onion powder	2 tsp. minced onion
1 tsp. dry mustard	1 Tbsp. prepared mustard
1 clove garlic	1/8 tsp. garlic powder
1 Tbsp. cornstarch	2 Tbsp. all purpose flour
2 large eggs	3 small eggs
1 cup honey	1¼ cups sugar plus ¼ cup water

EQUIVALENT WEIGHTS AND MEASURES

Food	Wt. or Count	Measure
Apples	1 pound (3 med.)	3 cups, sliced
Bacon	8 slices cooked	½ cup, crumbled
Bananas	1 pound (3 med.)	2½ cups, sliced
Bread	1 1/2 slices	1 cup bread crumbs
Cheese:		
Cheddar	1 pound	4-5 cups, shredded
Cream	3 ounces	6 Tbsp.
Monterey Jack	1 pound	4-5 cups, shredded
Coconut, flaked	1 pound	5 cups
Cornmeal	1 pound	3 cups
Cream, whipping	1 cup	2 cups, whipped
Dates, pitted	1 pound	2-3 cups, chopped
Flour, all purp.	1 pound	4 cups
Graham crackers	16 crackers	1-1/3 cups crumbs
Lemon juice	1 medium	2-3 Tbsp.
Macaroni	1 cup (4 oz.)	2¼ cups, cooked
Milk:		
Evaporated	6-oz. can	¾ cup
Sweetened condensed	14-oz. can	1-1/3 cups
Mimiature marshmallows	½ pound	4½ cups

Food	Wt. or Count	Measure
Nuts, in shell:		
Peanuts	1 pound	2 cups, shelled
Pecans	1 pound	2¼ cups, shelled
Walnuts	1 pound	1-2/3 cups, shelled
Nuts, shelled:		
Almonds	1 pound 2 oz.	4 cups
Peanuts	1 pound	4 cups
Pecans	1 pound	4 cups
Walnuts	1 pound	3 cups
Orange juice	1 medium	1/3 cup
Potatoes	2 pounds	6 medium
Raisins	1 pound	3 cups
Rice	1 cup	4 cups, cooked
Spaghetti	7 ounces	4 cups, cooked
Sugar:		
Brown	1 pound	2¼ cups
Powdered	1 pound	3½ cups
Granulated	1 pound	2 cups

THE LAZY COOK® recipes are the next easiest meals to peanut butter and crackers!

Index